*dark*water
A PASTOR'S MEMOIR *of* DEPRESSION AND FAITH

Michael J. Scholtes

Boyle
&
Dalton

Book Design & Production:
Boyle & Dalton
www.BoyleandDalton.com

Copyright © 2022 by
Michael J. Scholtes
LCCN: 2022902673

All rights reserved.
This book, or parts thereof, may not be
reproduced in any form without permission.

Scripture quotations are from New Revised Standard Version
Bible, copyright © 1989 National Council of the Churches
of Christ in the United States of America.
Used by permission. All rights reserved worldwide.

Some of the names and details in this book have been changed
for clarity and to protect the privacy of others.

Paperback ISBN: 978-1-63337-601-4
E-Book ISBN: 978-1-63337-602-1

Printed in the United States of America
1 3 5 7 9 10 8 6 4 2

PRAISE FOR DARKWATER

Take a risk and walk alongside Michael as he struggles with devastating self-messages, as he climbs a tree with a noose in his hand and gathers courage to become vulnerable again and again. It is estimated that in the United States, two thirds of all cases of depression are undiagnosed. Michael and all those with the courage to tell their stories are beginning to reduce this number.

—*Deacon Terry Lieb, National Board-Certified Counselor, Licensed PA Mental Health Counselor, Retired Executive Director, Diakon Family Life Services*

Pastor Scholtes has captured the voice of depression, a major mental disorder, through the richness of his metaphors, poetry, and personal narrative—a narrative that took courage to write. Anyone who wants to understand what depression is like needs to read this book, including pastors and laypersons alike. Through his journey, which is clearly rooted in a deep spiritual struggle, he tells us several crucial things about the illness. First, the negative impact of stigma. He captures elegantly how stigma, the fear of letting others know, compounds the illness leading to isolation. Second, the importance of support. The last thing someone needs is to be abandoned, to fend for oneself. Family, friends, the church family all have an important role in healing. Third, the importance of treatment. Treatment, which does not always "cure" completely, provides an important pathway for hope, a way to manage the dark voices of depression. Finally, even devout religious persons are not immune to mental disorders, and spiritual guidance can be an effective tool toward healing. I highly recommend this book.

—*Dennis E. Schell, Ph.D. Assistant Professor of Psychology, The George Washington University*

Get ready. *Darkwater is* Michael Scholtes' authentic, meticulous, and intimate account of his unrelenting confrontation with depression.

We get to follow this confrontation from his childhood to middle-age. Michael pulls back the curtain so we see him—son of a minister, floundering adolescent, bright student, restless pastor—stripped of pretension and laying out his life journey in a way that's as close to "in your face" as it gets without being cocky.

There is a stubborn fire in him that, after every triumph over its searing effort to rage uncontrolled, rekindles and repeatedly threatens to destroy the restored landscape of his grace-hungry soul. As Michael's bishop, I held my breath often while reading his story.

Darkwater is Michael's attempt to be honest with the world, with God, and with those in his life. When you put the book down, what makes it a satisfying read is not a happy ending, but the realization that what makes Michael strong against the depression is that he lays claim to and has learned to value the humanity, the honesty, the stubbornness, the pain, the will to persevere, the guilt, and the love that always came his way.

It's clear: while it came at a price, the renewal of his life journey is real.

—*Rev. Dr. Samuel R. Zeiser, Bishop Emeritus,*
Northeastern PA Synod of the Evangelical Lutheran Church in America

Michael Scholtes has given us a gift through this poignant memoir of one pastor's journey with depression. His writing is evocative, raw, creative, and poetic. If you suffer from depression, his story may give voice to your own struggles. If you want to understand what it looks like to live with depression, Scholtes has opened the door to his soul and invites you inside. Wading into *Darkwater* will reveal a depth of reflection, faith, and honesty that is rare and needed for those wanting to understand the inner world of mental illness.

—*Rev. Dr. Leah Schade, Assistant Professor of Preaching and Worship,*
Lexington Theological Seminary

Darkwater artfully captures the reality of an individual living with a mental illness. Scholtes masterfully highlights the delicate balance that occurs at the intersection of his faith, mental health, and mental illness. In a society where individuals battling mental illnesses are shunned and highly misunderstood, Scholtes shows great courage in sharing the true nature of his internal struggles. The book captured my curiosity and drew me in with the author's relatable style and coming-of-age authenticity. Entertaining and stimulating from cover to cover!

—*F. Dave Williams, licensed clinical social worker*

FOR JANE, WHO HELPED ME SEE THE
DARKWATER FOR WHAT IT TRULY WAS.

TABLE OF CONTENTS

INTRODUCTION I

PART ONE: A MIRROR DIMLY
CHAPTER 1:   WAKING THE BEAR 1
CHAPTER 2:   THE CARE TEAM 7
CHAPTER 3:   AWARDS NIGHT. 17
CHAPTER 4:   A POEM 23
CHAPTER 5:   THE MIKE TREATMENT 27
CHAPTER 6:   THE FINAL CUT (PART ONE). 33
CHAPTER 7:   THE POEM IN MY WALLET 39
CHAPTER 8:   FRESHMAN POETRY 43
CHAPTER 9:   TURN ON, TUNE IN, DEVOUT 47

PART TWO: DELIVER US FROM EVIL
CHAPTER 10: FURTHER FROM FINE 53
CHAPTER 11: THE FINAL CUT (PART TWO) 57
CHAPTER 12: IT WASN'T MONO. 65
CHAPTER 13: DAYS OF HOPE 71

PART THREE: CHASING AFTER WIND
CHAPTER 14: TWO MORE POEMS. 81
CHAPTER 15: STANDING OUTSIDE A BROKEN COLLEGE HOUSE
             WITH MY WALKMAN IN MY HAND 85
CHAPTER 16: GNAWING 89
CHAPTER 17: ONE CRAZY EMAIL 93
CHAPTER 18: NOW AND AGAIN 99
CHAPTER 19: THE SPECIAL GUEST .103

CHAPTER 20:	NOT THE BEST MAN 109
CHAPTER 21:	HOT AND BOTHERED 115
CHAPTER 22:	LOCKED IN 123

PART FOUR: KEEP AWAKE

CHAPTER 23:	THE BELLY OF THE WHALE 131
CHAPTER 24:	NEGATIVE NOLAN 139
CHAPTER 25:	ANNUNCIATION. 147
CHAPTER 26:	O'ER BETHLEHEM 157
CHAPTER 27:	MY SHADOW, MY SOUL MATE. 163
CHAPTER 28:	CUTTING THE CORD 167
CHAPTER 29:	ASKING FOR A CUP OF COLD WATER. 175
CHAPTER 30:	MOMENT OF FIRE. 181
CHAPTER 31:	NAMING YOUR SUFFERING 185
CHAPTER 32:	UNRECONCILED 193

INTERRUPTION: WORLD WITHOUT END. 205

PART FIVE: BE STILL

CHAPTER 33:	HOW TO CHANGE A TIRE 211
CHAPTER 34:	DARK NIGHT 217
CHAPTER 35:	THE TEXTURE OF DEPRESSION 221
CHAPTER 36:	DARKWATER 227
CHAPTER 37:	ANOINTED 233
CHAPTER 38:	HOME AT ST. DAVID'S 239
CHAPTER 39:	HIDDEN IN CHRIST WITH GOD 247
CHAPTER 40:	UNBIND HIM, AND LET HIM LOOSE 255

EPILOGUE: THE THORN OF PAUL 263

ACKNOWLEDGMENTS. 267
ABOUT THE AUTHOR. 271

INTRODUCTION

Darkwater is, in one way, the story of my relationship with God. My relationship with God began with water. I was a little over a month old when water was poured over my head and I was baptized. I obviously didn't understand my baptism that day. But baptism is just the beginning. Church was a major part of my childhood, and I slowly learned about baptism as I grew. I learned that baptism was a gift of God's grace. I learned that to Lutherans like me, grace is God's love freely given. One of the reasons why Lutherans practice infant baptism is because it is a beautiful sign of God's grace; infants have accomplished no great deeds and have done no great works, yet they receive this gift just the same.

Lutherans are Christians who trace their history to the sixteenth-century Protestant Reformation that was started by Martin Luther. I am a member of the Evangelical Lutheran Church in America (ELCA), the largest Lutheran denomination in the United States.

Lutherans teach that God's grace is *all gift*. We instill that you don't have to do the right things to earn God's love. You don't have to pray the right way to earn God's love. You don't have to believe the right things to earn God's love. To Lutherans, grace means that God's love is simply *there*, abundant and overflowing, pouring on us like the waters of baptism, our whole life long. We teach that striving to do the right thing is important, but not as a way to gain salvation; rather, it's a way of responding in gratitude for the salvation we've already received. Faith and prayer are important as well, but again, not to gain salvation but to live abundantly in the salvation we've already received.

Grace means that we are loved *unconditionally*. Grace means that God loves me, but not because I've done anything great, not because I've been a good person, not because I've obeyed the right laws, and not because I believe the right things. Grace means that God loves me—because that's who God is. God is the One who loves.

As I grew in the church, I learned more deeply about grace as I swam deeper and deeper into the waters of the baptism that started it all. I'm now middle-aged, and I am a parish pastor, preaching and teaching about grace myself.

Darkwater is also the story of my relationship with depression. Throughout my life I have lived with depression, an illness of the brain that sometimes takes away my ability to be happy, my ability to concentrate, and my ability to find joy or meaning in life. My depression is not constant; it ebbs and flows. I don't know what caused it, but it's been there since childhood. I have what is sometimes called "functional depression" or "smiling depression." That means that even when I'm sick, even when I'm at the lowest point, I am still able to get up in the morning, still able to do my job, and still able to preach. I have learned to hide it pretty well, but behind the mask, I am frequently an emotional train wreck, racked with guilt and despair.

I often experience my depression as a voice telling me that I am *not* a good person. I am *not* worthy of love—not from myself, not from anyone else, and not from God. And this is where my experience with depression collides with the faith I cherish and teach.

One way I think about this collision is through the lens of something Martin Luther wrote about: *simul iustus et peccator*. This is a Latin phrase that is usually translated as "simultaneously saint and sinner." We are sinners through and through. We have messed up and done the wrong thing repeatedly. And if we tried to justify ourselves before God based on our actions, we would fail. All of us would. But this phrase also means that we are able to do good things every day in the service of God and of one another. Through the death and resurrection of Jesus, God has forgiven us all, washed us clean, and made us holy. It's a dichotomy: we are broken and sinful, and we are saved, beloved, and holy.

Simul iustus et peccator. I preach and teach this, and I believe it. To me, it's part of talking about grace. Even when depressed, I still teach and preach grace. I also believe it for everybody else, but when depression kicks up, I find that I don't believe it for me. I don't believe that I am a *iustus* (saint) at all. In those times, I believe that I am the exception to the rule that God loves everyone. I have no trouble remembering that I am a *peccator* (sinner)—depraved, worthless, unloved, and unlovable.

They say the devil knows scripture as well as any saint, and he can twist and misuse it. Depression is my own personal devil in this way, a dark voice who speaks in my head. I use "voice" as a metaphor here as I don't actually hear voices like some people do. Perhaps it's my own voice echoing around my own head, but thanks to whatever brain chemistry has caused the depression, my own voice can be very self-destructive.

Darkwater is the story of the voices I hear—the voice of depression and the voice of faith.

PART ONE
A MIRROR DIMLY

CHAPTER 1
WAKING THE BEAR

AGE 11

They tried to scare me that night—and they did. But it wasn't the fright they were planning. It was the early stirrings of a beast that would frighten me for decades to come.

"All right, lights out!"

All the flashlights went out. A few of the boys had been shining their lights on the top tarp, pretending their flashlights were lightsabers. It was the mid-1980s, and I was at church camp with my best friend, Ryan. He held one of the flashlights. I didn't know if he was on the side of the Empire or the Rebellion, or even if there were such sides here. Their game made no sense, but I was enjoying watching the cooler kids play while lying in my sleeping bag on the edge of the tarp.

I was uncomfortable but not just from the rock in my back. I enjoyed coming to camp every year with Ryan, and I slept okay most nights in the cabins. But I knew I wouldn't sleep well tonight. This was the "overnight." Earlier that day, our coed group of about fifteen kids and two counselors hiked out into the woods. We found a spot, set up a huge tarp on the ground, and hung another tarp over it in case of rain. We played games, cooked over a campfire we made, and once night came, we gathered under the tarp to sleep. All the kids were in their sleeping bags whispering to each other while the counselors stayed up at the campfire about fifty yards away.

A light appeared on the top tarp. I heard one of the other boys laughing. Then another light, and the two began to attack each another. More laughter.

"I said lights out!" Our counselor Bill was about twenty years old with a straggly beard. I kept my mouth shut and my flashlight off, but I didn't mind watching the others play their game. At least it distracted me from that rock poking into my back.

"Ryan, can you move over at all?" I whispered. His sleeping bag was right next to mine.

"Sorry, dude," he said, "I'm squished in here too. What's wrong?"

"Rock in my back," I said.

In the dim light that flickered from the campfire, I could see him smile. "Again? Is that the same rock as last year, or the one from two years ago?"

"Shut up," I said, and I rolled over in pain.

It was around this time that the other boys decided that fart noises were more important than *Star Wars*. The girls were not impressed. "Eww! Shut up!"

I closed my eyes and smiled.

After a few minutes, the boys quieted down. All I could hear were the sounds of insects in the woods and the crackling of the fire. Then there was a louder crackling sound, like someone breaking a large stick in half. I thought maybe the counselors were putting more wood in the fire. But then I heard it again. And again. I could hear rustling from other sleeping bags.

One girl asked, "What is that sound?"

A boy replied, "I don't know." I opened my eyes but didn't sit up. I was facing away from everybody else, and I didn't want anybody to know I was awake.

The noise outside grew louder. It sounded like something large walking around. Under the tarp, the sounds of the group grew louder as well. It seemed like everybody was sitting up, trying to figure out what was happening.

Suddenly I heard something running toward the tarp, and a few girls screamed.

"Shhh!" said a voice outside. It was Bill. He said, "I think there's a bear nearby." I kept my eyes closed tight and didn't move. I did not want anyone to know I was awake. I did not want to deal with this, not tonight, not out in the woods, not with this rock under me.

The noises outside grew louder. Crack. Crunch. There was definitely something large out there, and quite possibly more than one something. Everyone under the tarp was freaking out. Bill kept saying things like, "You've got to keep quiet," and, "It can smell your fear." My teeth were grinding. I took shallow breaths through my nose. I was willing the tears not to come. This was too much. This was not a bear. This was something else, something stronger, something coming for me.

"*Yahhhhhh!*" I heard a voice outside, a human voice yelling—then more yells as a group of campers a year or two older came rushing into the tarp. One of them stepped on my hair. I still pretended I was sleeping. More screaming broke out from the girls with a few more screams from the boys. And then—laughter. Everybody started laughing. The older kids. The younger kids. Bill and the other counselors. Even the camp chaplain was there laughing. It was all a prank.

I sat up, seething. I got out of my sleeping bag, put my shoes on, and stood up. I shouted, "That's a lousy trick to play on a manic-depressive!" and stomped out from under the tarp. I walked toward the fire and sat down on a rock.

Yeah. That's really what I said. Eleven years old, and I knew the term "manic-depressive." Now, I had never received such a diagnosis. I had never been to a psychiatrist or a counselor. Not at that point. But I was always a smart kid with a brain that worked overtime. I read all the time, devouring books, magazines, and anything I could get my hands on. Somewhere in that reading I came across the term manic-depressive, and I immediately latched onto it.

What a beautiful phrase, I thought. I assumed I understood what it meant. I thought it was somebody who was moody, somebody who was really happy sometimes and really angry and sad at other times. That certainly described me. I loved that phrase. It made me feel special. Like there was something wrong with me. Like I was a victim. It made me unique and brought me attention. And I had no problem throwing it around like a weapon.

The laughing stopped. I looked back and saw the counselors and the chaplain talking to each other, gesturing toward me. Yep, there was the attention I always sought. It didn't feel good, though; it felt dry and jagged in my throat. I looked over at the tarp and saw Ryan standing there talking with one of the other boys. The other boy was pointing at me, and Ryan nodded, shook his head, and shrugged his shoulders. Ryan and I made eye contact. He mouthed the word "Dude," then tilted his head a little. I thought he was trying to ask me, *Why did you do that? Why do you always make things so hard for yourself?* Ryan could never understand why I did things like this. I didn't respond. He gave me the tiniest smile, turned, and went back under the tarp.

I sat there on that rock with tears on the edge of emerging. I could feel the rage, the blood pumping behind my eyes. I didn't know if I was angry at the older campers, the counselors, or myself. Definitely myself, I decided, but maybe them too. Oh, but unquestionably myself. I should not have said what I said. I should not have done this. I should have known better. *I should have known better.*

Bill walked over to the tarp and tried to get the others to pipe down and get back in bed. One of the other counselors, Lucy, came and sat next to me. She started talking. I was staring into the distance, and I only heard snippets of what she said. ". . . it was just supposed to be a fun prank . . . I'm sorry that it upset you . . . if you want to talk . . . go back and try to get some sleep . . ."

Once I realized that she was trying to get me to go back to the tarp, I nodded and walked back. The other kids were quiet now except for some whispering. I crawled in my sleeping bag and lay down. I couldn't sleep, just as I'd predicted. After a while, the whispering around me stopped, and the distant voices of the counselors stopped. But I didn't notice. I was listening to another voice who was just clearing his throat.

CHAPTER 2
THE CARE TEAM

AGE 14

I shivered in the cold, huddled in a group with four other ninth graders. This was what it was like every morning in junior high school. The buses spit us out, and we glommed together in these pods of four or five, waiting for the school doors to open. Rain or shine, hot or cold. On this cold morning as I made small talk, I felt like I was being watched. Out of the corner of my eye, I thought I saw two girls in another pod looking at me and pointing. I turned, and they looked away. The doors opened at last, and we all shuffled inside.

I threw my coat and hat in my locker and slipped into homeroom. My eyes shot around as I counted three—no, four—people staring at me, just like the girls outside. I gingerly touched my hair. Had I forgotten to brush it? I examined my clothing. Nothing was torn or stained. What was all this attention about? I sat down at my desk and stewed about what was going on. I'd been absent the day before. Had I missed something important?

I was still thinking about this when the bell rang to go to first period. I got up and was heading toward the door when I heard my friend Amanda call my name. She grabbed my arm and said, "We need to talk. I'll tell you about it when we get to class." Amanda and I had the same first period history class with Mr. Orloski, so I was hopeful we could talk before class started.

I hurried to Mr. Orloski's room, but Amanda didn't walk in the door until just before the bell rang. Mr. Orloski walked in behind her, ruining pre-class conversation time. But just as Amanda sat down, she tossed a piece of paper that was folded into a small triangle onto my desk. I opened the paper on top of my history notebook. I didn't bother being surreptitious—Mr. Orloski was so old and absentminded he'd never notice anyway. The note said:

Scholtie,

You missed quite a health class yesterday. Ryan and I were talking about you, about some of your "quirks," and since we sit up front, Mrs. Spicer overheard us. She asked us some questions, and before we knew it, other kids joined in. We mentioned how you get moody and how you used to talk about being manic-depressive. I didn't realize what was going on until I saw Mrs. Spicer writing some things down in a notebook. I think she might be activating the Care Team. I'm really sorry. I wasn't trying to be mean.

Amanda

Oh, lovely. Just lovely. So that's why people had been staring at me. What had been said in health class? As I stared at the words on Amanda's note, I looked around the class, picturing all these people—the jocks, the cool kids, the other nerds—all talking about me. Oh, God. What had they said? This was not good. I had to either never miss school again, or never come back again. How could I even look anyone in the eye now?

And even better—the Care Team. I had the other students *and* the teachers talking about me. We had learned about the Care Team a few months earlier. It was a new program designed to show that the school "cared" about us. The team was made up of the school nurse, the guidance counselor, and a few teachers (including Mrs. Spicer). They tried to identify students in need—kids who were involved in drug abuse, who had trouble at home, who had some sort of mental illness, or who had anything else going on that might cause them to be in need of intervention. The team would then try to connect these students with appropriate resources in an effort to help them.

Anybody, including students, could refer someone to the Care Team, and it looked like I had been publicly referred the previous day. Lovely. Just lovely. I thought about walking out of the class, down the hall, out the front door of the school, down the road, out of town, over the mountain, and across the state line. How far was it to Canada?

I folded up the note slowly and put it in the pocket of my jeans. I looked over at Amanda. She bit her bottom lip as she looked at me, asking me silently for absolution. I quickly wrote *It's okay* on my notebook and turned the notebook toward her so she could read it. But I didn't know if it was okay. How could I?

An hour later, I was in English class. I was normally a good student, but that day I couldn't focus. I couldn't pay attention to anything Mr. Novak was saying. All I could think about was what everyone else in class thought of me. It felt like my stomach was twisting itself into a double helix. Then I saw a red-haired student walk into the classroom. She approached Mr. Novak and handed him a note. He read it while she stood waiting. He looked up and said, "Michael." He motioned me forward and told me to go with the girl. As I walked out, I shrugged at Amanda. I followed the redhead silently as she led me to the nurse's office. "Thanks," I muttered as she silently turned and walked away.

This was the first time I'd been in the nurse's office. It was cold and clinical with pale green walls, a desk up against one wall, a bed against another wall, and a round stool. The bed looked hard and uncomfortable. The nurse was hunched over her desk, sitting on one of those office chairs that can spin. She heard me come in, and without looking said, "Michael, you can sit down." I sat on the stool. It wobbled and spun a bit as I sat, and I thought about pulling it into the middle of the room and spinning in circles.

She finally looked up and turned her head from the desk to face me, observing me over the top of wide-rimmed glasses that sat on her nose. She sat up taller and spun her chair toward me. She pushed up her glasses and said, "So, I'd like to talk with you for a few minutes." I nodded.

She picked up a notebook and a pen and held them loosely in her hands. "How are things at home?" she asked.

"Fine."

"How is your schoolwork?" she asked.

"Fine."

"Do you have a job?" she asked.

"I do odd jobs at my neighbor's house. That's about it."

"Do you drink?" she asked.

"You mean like . . . alcohol?"

She nodded but didn't say anything.

"Umm, no. I've never tried it, except for communion at church."

Her pen slashed something in her notebook. "How about drugs?"

I was floored. For all my moodiness, I was really an innocent and straightedge kind of kid. I said, "I don't even know where to get them. Never."

Her pen moved again with a flourish. She looked up at me, pursed her lips, and nodded slightly. Then she sighed and said, "Okay. Thank you for coming in. Here's a note to get back to class." She scribbled something on a slip of paper and handed it to me. I walked out and headed slowly back to class, shaking my head as I went. I did not like this. This was not okay. This was seriously not okay. I felt attacked. The opening narration to the television show *The A-Team* popped into my head: "In 1972, a crack commando unit was sent to prison by a military court for a crime they didn't commit." But I was no Mr. T. I had no idea how I'd get out of this. I just hoped it was over. As I walked up the stairs, I stopped on a landing and looked longingly out the window. Canada wasn't too far away, was it?

The next day, I was in Mr. Novak's English class again, and the same taciturn red-haired student came in with another note. Mr. Novak looked at it and said, "Michael," and motioned for me to follow her again. This time she led me to the guidance counselor's office. "Moving up in the world?" I said to her. She smiled and walked back toward the main office without saying a word.

The counselor looked up from his desk, saw me at the doorway, and got up. He said, "Hello Mike. Come on in. Can I call you Mike, or do you prefer Michael?" He shook my hand and led me to a comfortable chair.

I looked around. This room was very different from the nurse's office. The walls were painted the same nasty pale green, but whereas that green had looked sterile in the nurse's office, here it seemed old and worn. The furniture was wooden and seemed worn as well. Faded paintings lined the walls. It felt like an old cabin, lived-in and loved, but not particularly well maintained.

The counselor sat opposite me and said, "Thank you for coming in. I'd like to talk with you about a few things." He stopped abruptly and looked up. "I'm sorry," he said, "I didn't hear your answer before. May I call you Mike, or Michael, or . . ."

"Mike is fine."

He smiled. "Good. Mike, what's your home life like? Tell me about your family."

"Well, my father's a pastor, and my mother teaches piano. I have a sister who's in sixth grade."

He nodded. "Tell me about what a typical evening looks like in your house."

"Well, I get home from school, and my mother is already teaching a lesson. She teaches for a few hours in the afternoon and evening. I usually get a snack and then go up to my room and do my homework. Then I'll go for a walk in the woods or maybe just watch TV in my room, and then I'll go down and get some supper."

The counselor interrupted. "Do you eat together as a family?"

I shook my head. "No, that just doesn't work with my mom's schedule. She always cooks during the day and puts it in the fridge for us. We each just microwave our supper when we want to. Anyway, then for the rest of the night I'm usually watching TV or talking on the phone with somebody. Or maybe writing a letter to someone."

"Sounds lonely," he said.

I shrugged. "I don't feel lonely."

He frowned for a fraction of a second and then said, "Do you have a lot of friends?"

"I have a few good ones: Amanda and Ryan. I don't know. Maybe that's about it."

This went on for some time. The comfortable atmosphere of the room began to feel stifling and tight. I did not like this. The counselor kept asking question after question, and I kept answering them. But I was paying more attention to what was happening inside me. I felt like this was my fault. I had brought this on myself. I should have known better. This was all because of the way I acted, the way I talked, the stupid things I said sometimes. If I would just have kept my mouth shut, I wouldn't be here.

A nasty voice from deep inside began to growl and grumble. *You think you're so smart, but you're not. You really stepped in it this time.* I told the voice, *I'm sorry.* This internal conversation must have taken a while, because the next thing I heard was this:

"So what do you think?" the counselor asked. "Do you think you could join a gym?"

The voice in my head got quiet. It must have been as dumbstruck as I was. I knew I had zoned out, but how did we get to the idea of a gym? Was it something to do with exercise being helpful? Or what? Why did he suggest that? No, I was certainly not going to join a gym just because a guidance counselor said so. What a strange man.

"I guess," I mumbled.

"Okay. Well, I will see you again next week. We'll keep this conversation going." He stood up and offered his hand. I shook it limply. "Until next time," he said, smiling.

I walked out of the office numb. I did not want this attention. *You don't deserve attention,* the voice whispered. I didn't want help, not this way. *You don't need help.* I didn't want to join a gym. *Waste of time.* I didn't want to meet with the guidance counselor again. *Waste of time.* I was not happy about this at all. This was seriously, seriously not okay.

That evening, after her piano lessons ended, I talked to my mother. We sat in the kitchen, the place where all important conversations happened in that house. We sat across from each other at the round wooden table, the sound of the dishwasher sloshing as we talked. I told her what Amanda had written in her note. I told her about the meetings with the nurse and the guidance counselor. I told her about the Care Team. I didn't want to cry. I didn't intend to cry. But my voice kept cracking as I shared all this news, and I knew the tears weren't far away.

My mother listened. Then she said calmly, "Well, I can understand why they'd think that. The way you talk sometimes. You talked about suicide when you were ten."

"But I never meant it! I just wanted attention!" I pleaded.

"And now you've got it."

"And I don't want it! I'm not suicidal. And I'm not on drugs. You believe me, don't you?" I asked, pleading.

She paused, looking intently at me. Then she said, "Yes."

"I can't take this anymore. I just want it to stop." I put my head down on the table, and a day's worth of pent-up tears flowed out.

My mother put her hand on my shoulder and said, "I'll call the school. I'll get this straightened out."

The next day, she did. She spoke to the guidance counselor and told him that these meetings were starting to get me depressed. He said, "I'd rather have a depressed Michael than no Michael at all." Nonetheless, she prevailed, and I never met with him again.

I heard from the Care Team one last time. After my mom's calls to the school, I was called out of class, this time to go speak to my math teacher. He was one of my favorite teachers, and I knew that he liked me too. I also knew that he was on the Care Team.

He stepped out of his classroom and talked with me in the hall. He said something like, "Mike, is everything all right?"

I smiled and told him, "I'm not suicidal or on drugs, Mr. Morgan."

He smiled, put his hand on my shoulder, and said, "Good. I didn't think so." He went back into his classroom.

Thank God that was over.

CHAPTER 3
AWARDS NIGHT

AGE 14

I walked into my junior high school with my parents and led them to the auditorium. It was so strange to be there in the evening, so strange to be there with Mom and Dad. We walked past acquaintances of mine, and I said hello. But I was not in any mood to talk to them. I didn't want my parents there. I didn't want to be there at all.

We reached the auditorium and were greeted by the smell of the old wood floor and the sound of the creaky folding chairs. The room was so loud. Whoever designed it must have loved the echo of hundreds of teenagers. An usher handed us programs and pointed my parents to the back where they would sit. I was directed to the middle of the room, where I saw lots of other students. I approached slowly, looking around to see if there was anyone I actually wanted to sit next to. My heart leapt when I saw Amanda waving to me. Oh, thank God.

She was saving a seat for me. Maybe this wouldn't be as bad as I expected. I sat down next to her and sighed.

Amanda turned to me and asked, "So, who's going to be the big winner tonight?"

I was confused. "What?"

She opened her eyes wide and said, "Really? Don't be stupid. You know. Who's going to get the most awards tonight? It's not me. It'll either be you or Clara."

I leaned back in the chair and said, "I don't know. I hope it's her."

"Hey. What's wrong?"

"Nothing," I said.

She nodded. "Yeah, nothing. Just being Mike, right?"

"Sure. Hey, don't call the Care Team, okay?"

I closed my eyes, and then Amanda poked me. She had her program open in her hand. "Look," she said. "This is the best name for an award." She pointed to a line that read *The American Legion Most Outstanding Boy and Most Outstanding Girl awards.* She smiled and said, "I hope you're the most outstanding boy, Scholtie."

"Shut up." I was starting to sweat. It was so hot in there. It was unseasonably warm for early June, and the school was not air-conditioned. Between the noise and the heat, I was so ready for this to be over.

The principal walked out on the stage and asked for everyone to be quiet. And it started. Dozens and dozens of awards were handed out. My name got called for Biology Achievement, World History Achievement, Math Achievement, and Presidential Academic Fitness Award. I got up each time, walked to the stage each time, received a piece of paper each time, and sat back down next to Amanda each time. She was keeping track of the standings; Clara and I were neck and neck.

I knew this would happen. Every year it happened. I always got a bunch of awards because I always had outstanding grades. I had been the "whiz kid" since kindergarten. I was always top of the class. I never had to work hard for it. It just came easily to me. School smarts were always a gift I had.

But every time awards were given out, something felt wrong about it. I never felt proud or happy at these things—I felt awkward and confused instead. For a time, I tried to explain those feelings as a sense that these awards should be given for effort, and I knew that I didn't put nearly as much effort into schoolwork as other students.

As I sat in the junior high auditorium that evening, the feelings were even more intense than usual. They started to coalesce into a bitter thought, into a single word: *Fraud!* Every time I heard my name announced, I felt as though a voice in my head were shouting out, *Fraud!*

Every time I walked toward the stage, I felt something like a squeezing around my head, like a clutching in my chest. It was as though a voice were telling me, *You don't belong here. You are a fraud. They don't know who you really are. If they did, they would never have given this to you. You will never fulfill your potential. You are a sham. A con artist. A poseur.*

None of this was rational. I hadn't cheated or faked my way to anything. I had earned those awards honestly. But those feelings were so strong that I couldn't hear the voice of reason at all that night.

Then the final awards: The American Legion Most Outstanding Boy and Most Outstanding Girl. Amanda was called as runner-up for Most Outstanding Girl. Clara was the winner. They were both still on stage as the runner-up for Most Outstanding Boy was announced. It was a kid named Gary who wasn't at the ceremony. I closed my eyes, my teeth clenched. And then I heard two voices together. From the stage, I heard my name being called. From inside myself, I heard my other names: *Fraud. Liar. Imbecile. Pretender.*

I should be clear that this voice was never a literal voice—it's more like a part of the internal monologue that we all have. It's never been a hallucination. I've never had trouble telling this voice apart from other people. But I have often had trouble distinguishing this voice from myself.

I stood up and walked on stage for the final time that night. Amanda smiled at me and mouthed the word "tie." I walked to the American Legion representatives and accepted their fraudulent, misguided award. I didn't smile or even say "thank you." I just stood there next to the others. We were still all on stage as Mr. Decker announced that the ceremony was over, that everyone was invited to take photos now, and that we could then head to the cafeteria for refreshments.

The newspaper photographer started taking photographs of us in groups. I heard the voice say, *Great. Now the whole town will see you, Fraud.* I wanted to be somewhere else. Maybe if I got away from the awards, away from the school, this feeling would go away.

After photographs were over, I found my parents and asked if we could go home.

"Don't you want to talk with your friends for a few minutes?" they asked.

No, I didn't. I couldn't pay attention to my friends anyway. I could only focus on my feelings. I didn't even say goodbye to Amanda. I just had to go.

When we arrived home, I said goodnight, went right to my room, and sat down on the bed.

You didn't deserve any of that. Look how much faith they put in you. You will seriously disappoint them.

I got under the covers and lay there, listening to the voice's dark lullaby.

CHAPTER 4
A POEM

AGE 14

In tenth grade, I had a big yellow spiral-bound notebook. I used it as a journal, and I also started to scribble poetry in it. This is one of my earliest poems. I never gave it a name. The only thing written above it was the date. Bear with me here—I am well aware that it's terrible. It's not presented as a work of art, but rather an artifact of what I was feeling at the time.

> **12.4.90**
> My name is Michael
> I am an instrument
> God's peace tries to work
> Through me, tries
> But fails
> At times I am good
> At others I disgust

Even myself
I say I believe in Christ
But do I?
I don't know
Sometimes, sometimes
I feel the Spirit in me
Trying, struggling to come out
But it is banished
Banished by fear
Fear of unknowns
Fear of nonconformity
Fear of being holy
I fear God, but not
The way I should
I fear God will enter me
Make my life meaningful
Banish my ego to abysses unknown
My ego is me
Loss of it frightens me
Loss of ego is gain of eternal life
Why does eternal life scare me?
Lack of trust
If there is no God, why bother
Ego is a fun thing to have
If I have one life I would rather share it with my ego
Than devote it to a nonexistent God
But God is extant
I feel His presence
He loves me

How
How
How can I deny him so?
I need help
God help me
To love you and raise your name
While lowering mine
Let your Holy Spirit enter me
I love you God
I will try
My name is Michael
My Father is God

I didn't know it at the time, but I was living Romans 7:15 where Paul writes, "I do not understand my own actions. For I do not do what I want, but I do the very thing I hate."

I didn't realize as a teenager that doubt and worry are always a part of faith. Faith is never perfect on this side of the grave; faith is a messy, tentative thing. The life of faith is not a pristine, perfectly moral, and happy life. Look at the apostles—confused and delirious, yet they were the leaders of the church. Look at the archetypal king of Israel, David—a murderer and an adulterer, yet God's most faithful leader. Look at Paul himself—first a persecutor of Christians, then a tireless evangelist who loved nothing more than being in prison. Anne Lamott wrote, "The opposite of faith is not doubt, but certainty." Doubt, confusion, inconsistency—all are part of the life of faith.

CHAPTER 5
THE MIKE TREATMENT

AGE 15

We were sitting on the bed in her bedroom. Her parents weren't home, but they knew I was there, and they trusted us. Why did they trust us? I don't know. Robin and I had been dating for about three months. She was a year behind me in school, but we hadn't met there; we met at church camp. And we were madly in love in that intense and earnest way that only "emo" teenagers can be. We talked on the phone every night and saw each other every weekend. We sometimes talked about what it would be like when we were married. I knew, absolutely knew, that she was "the one."

Of course, Robin was not the first "one," nor would she be the last. I hadn't yet forgotten about Melissa, the first "one." Melissa and I met about a year earlier at an event called Youth Convo, a Lutheran youth event for teenagers all over northeastern Pennsylvania. It was held in conjunction with the annual Synod

Assembly, where clergy and other adult leaders met over three days to discuss church business. While the grown-ups voted and debated, the teenagers had an absolute blast. We were housed at a college campus for the weekend, and we sang songs, played games, had Bible studies, built relationships, and always, always had a dance. Events like this were commonplace in the Northeastern Pennsylvania Synod at the time, and I tried to attend them all.

I developed a crush on Melissa immediately. I adored her enthusiasm and her laugh. I was smitten by the way her voice cracked when she got excited. And the best part—she seemed to like me too. When the dance arrived, I couldn't wait for the first slow song. It was "Heaven" by Bryan Adams. I asked Melissa if she wanted to dance. She looked in my eyes and said, "Of course!"

I smiled and put my hands on her waist, expecting that we would stand a few feet apart and do the "eighth-grade shuffle," as we called it back home. She said quietly, "Stop it. Come on." She pulled me closer, wrapped her arms around my neck, and laid her head on my shoulder. I started to understand that the "heaven" Bryan Adams was singing about wasn't the same one that I read about in the Bible.

After the dance ended, it was time to go back to our respective rooms for the night. We entered the elevator together, and when the door closed, Melissa pulled me close and kissed me. Really kissed me. She tasted like pretzels. When our lips parted, I said, "I love you."

She said, "You need to get some sleep."

But enough about Melissa. She wasn't the "one" anymore—Robin was. Robin and I were sitting on her bed, listening to a cassette of a Christian rock group we'd seen together a few weeks earlier. I lay down and looked over at her. "I don't know what you see in me," I said.

She smiled and replied, "I love you! That's what I see in you."

I knew that was wrong. It was just wrong. I shook my head. "No, I just don't understand. There's no reason you should love me. I'm completely worthless."

She grabbed my hand and said, "That's not true."

I pulled my hand away and rolled over, looking away from her. "Yes, it is. There is nothing worthwhile about me. I'm just going to hurt you."

"No. You're smart, you're funny, you're cute. I love the way you hug me."

My head felt tight. I knew that this was not true. I knew that I had to protect her from myself. I said, "No, I've just tricked you into thinking that. I'm worthless. I'm evil."

Robin crawled over me and put her face right in front of mine. "Stop this. Why are you saying this?"

I shouted, "Because it's true!"

She started to kiss me, but I pulled away. I blurted out, "No. I can't hurt you like this anymore. I have to leave."

Robin was quiet for a moment. I heard her get off the bed and sit on the floor, leaning against the wall. I could hear her starting to cry. Apart from that, everything was silent. The Christian rock cassette had reached its end and stopped with a loud *CLICK*.

Something snapped within me as I realized what I'd done. "Oh my God," I whispered quietly, quivering with each word. "I am so sorry." I sat up and looked at Robin. I saw the tears on her face and felt my own begin to stream. "I am so sorry. I don't know why I did that."

I got off the bed and walked over to Robin. I sat down next to her and said, "I am so sorry. I honestly don't know why I did that. You don't deserve that. You're amazing, and I love you, and I just . . ."

She sniffed, wiped her eyes, and said tenderly, "What? You just what?"

I sobbed a little, took a deep breath, and said, "I just can't believe I would do this to you. You are the most wonderful person and look how I treat you. I was right. I do hurt you." I looked at her. "See, you're crying. I just made you cry! Maybe I should leave."

"No," she said. She put her arms around me. "No, we'll get through this. Just like we did the last time you did this."

The last time I did this. That's the punch line, isn't it?

I did this so often that I gave it a name: the "Mike Treatment." It was this remarkably self-fulfilling pattern. I would tear myself down, telling my girlfriend over and over how terrible I was, knowing that I'd hear good things about myself in return. Then, once I'd gone too far, I'd stop and apologize profusely, only to then feel even more guilty. Sometimes the cycle would start again immediately. And it wasn't just with Robin. It was with every girlfriend I ever had in high school: Melissa, Cathy, and Colleen. "You shouldn't be with me," I'd always say. And after going through the Mike Treatment a few times, I suppose they all eventually decided I was right.

I still struggle to determine just what need I was fulfilling by performing the Mike Treatment. I can tell you what it felt like inside. In those moments, it felt as though I was acting on behalf of someone else. It felt as though I was playing a role. I felt as though there was someone else who was above me, or somehow wiser than me, who knew what was best, who was like some dark superego. This wise entity could see the future: somehow he knew that I would hurt Robin and that I was not able to prevent it. He knew that I was worthless and useless and deserved to be alone.

In those moments, he declared martial law on me. And he gave me a job to do. On behalf of the dark superego, it was my job to convince Robin how useless I really was. I wasn't interested in listening to her arguments. I was the prosecutor, not the jury. Nobody, not Robin or any of the others, could ever win these arguments. I was too good at it. And then at the end, the dark superego would disappear, and I was left alone wondering why I'd ever done this and what on earth I could do now to make it up to her.

I never wanted to hurt Robin or anyone else. Maybe I just wanted so much to hurt myself that I didn't care in those moments if others got hurt as well.

CHAPTER 6
THE FINAL CUT (PART ONE)

AGE 16

In the woods near my house, there was an old bridge over the Nescopeck Creek. They say that railroad cars once used it, but that was long ago, long before I lived there. That bridge was a fun spot. It wasn't really a walking bridge; it was just I-beams connecting two concrete trusses. The whole thing was about twenty feet across and ten feet wide. You could walk across the beams if you were careful. I had one friend who would routinely ride his dirt bike across it. That kid was brave.

The best part of that bridge was what was below it. Concrete trusses forced the river to become a waterfall spilling into a deep pool beneath the bridge. The neighborhood kids referred to this spot as "the Falls." I don't know when I learned it or who told me, but somehow I always knew that the water was ten feet deep at the Falls.

In my preteen years, a few of us would often sit on the bridge in the summer, legs dangling over the water. If it was warm enough, some of the kids would jump into the pool below. Me, I never had the guts to. Nonetheless, it was a place where I always felt free and part of the neighborhood group. Until I made the mistake of telling my parents how much fun it was. After that I was no longer allowed to play there because of undercurrents, the chance of hitting my head on one of the beams, that sort of thing. Of course, that didn't always stop me.

Years went by, and I stopped playing in the Falls. I grew out of it, but I still remembered it as a dangerous and alluring spot, a place my mother forbade me from going. I still recalled the ancient lore: "It's ten feet deep at the Falls." One day when I was sixteen, the memory of the Falls entered my mind, and I wondered how dangerous it was in reality. Was it really as I remembered? Could it be dangerous enough for what I had in mind? If all the stories were true, then it must be. Ten feet deep? That should do. Undercurrents? It would only help.

One April day after school, I put on my denim jacket and walked out of the house. *There is no other way out.* The air was chilly and damp. I wasn't sure this jacket was going to be warm enough, but I knew I'd feel warmer after walking for a few minutes. I walked down the road past the old apartments. Just past the rickety green bridge, I turned left into the woods that I knew so well, the woods where I played, where I walked, where I biked, and where I smoked. These were my stomping grounds, and this felt like the fitting place and the fitting way to do this.

The voice encouraged me. *Sure. Walk it one last time and enjoy it. Take the enjoyment. You don't deserve it, but who is it going to hurt to give yourself this one thing?*

I walked along the creek, listening to the water rushing, that sound I knew so well. I came to a row of boulders lined up along the creek edge, and I knew this was where I should cross. It was always shallow here. Besides, I didn't care if my feet got wet. I walked through the creek and kept walking on the faint trail. The sky was gray, and it lent a ghostly color to the newly budding trees. While I walked, I thought about why I was doing this. I thought about Cathy. She and I had been dating for four months, and so of course I was madly in love. But last week I got a letter from Lily. Lily was someone I met at camp two years earlier. We became friends, but I had hoped in the beginning for something more. I'd long given up on that thought, but now a letter . . .

The voice interjected. *Yes. That letter. That's why you're here. That's why we're doing this, why we're taking this walk. Because you can't decide what to do. And no matter what you do, you will hurt someone. Just like always. Keep walking.*

Oh, that letter. I couldn't believe that Lily actually liked me too. When we were on top of the mountain and I tried to put my arm around her, she'd pulled away—but she really wanted me to follow her. I couldn't believe she'd told me that in her letter. I couldn't believe she still felt the same way.

I can't do this, I thought. What about Cathy? I can't believe I care about this when I'm in love with Cathy.

A normal person wouldn't be like this. A normal person, a kind person, a compassionate person, a Christian, wouldn't be like this. A normal person would just file that letter away under "Isn't that interesting?" But not you.

What does this mean? I wondered. Was I cheating on Cathy just by having these thoughts?

You see? You're already hurting people, and you haven't even done anything yet.

Hold on, wait, I thought in return. That doesn't make sense—

Shut up! You're a scoundrel, a liar, a cheater, a complete waste of matter.

I started to cry and leaned against a tree. I couldn't do this. I looked up and realized that I knew this tree. This was the tree where I screamed last fall when I almost walked face first into a nest of webworms. As I stared at the tree, I remembered seeing hundreds of the squirming caterpillars inches from my face, just before I fell backward onto the ground in disgust and fear. I remembered that I turned back to the tree when I was a few yards away and thought how pretty the web looked from a distance. How odd that from far away it should seem so lovely, but up close so revolting.

Yes! That's it! That's exactly who you are! That's why nobody else can see you for what you really are. From a distance, you might seem harmless, but up close, you are terrible. You are worthless. You are selfish and arrogant and childish. You are a monster. You are a nightmare. You are the nightmare of the world.

I straightened, wiped the tears on my jacket, and kept walking, my jaw firm. I could see the ridge just up ahead where the railroad bed sat.

Cathy deserves better than you. Lily deserves better than you. You are a monster, and neither of them deserve that, and neither does the world. Just go. Go. Now.

I sprinted up the hill to the old railroad bed. I turned left. This was going to be the most selfless thing I'd ever done.

Maybe the only selfless thing you've ever done. So let's make up for lost time. Do the right thing.

When I got to the Falls, I started looking for some rocks.

I found two heavy ones, each about half the size of my head. That's what I wanted. I carried them up to the bridge and sat there looking down. I looked down at the water, about ten feet below me. It was chilly out, and I knew the water would be freezing. That would help too. I untied my shoes and took the laces out. I always wore high-top sneakers, which have absurdly long laces. I carefully tied one rock to each foot. I left the shoes on. Why not? What difference would it make, shoes or not?

This was it. I had to do this. *Do it.* It was for the betterment of the world. *Do it.*

I jumped.

In midair I changed my mind.

Luckily, my plan was not exactly foolproof.

I entered the water and went under. I hit bottom and lost my balance as the rocks slid over the mud at the bottom of the pool. My knees were bent, and I was almost lying on my back. I flailed, desperately trying to pull myself back up to the surface. As I thrashed about with the rocks, my feet still on the bottom, I felt my arms break the surface of the water.

I straightened myself up and found I was able to stand in this water—the water only reaching up to my torso. This "ten-foot-deep" pool was actually no more than three or four feet deep. I stood there for a moment, and then started to walk to the shore. There was certainly a current, but not the fatal undertow I'd been expecting. The rocks on my feet added some drag, but they didn't feel like the cement shoes I'd been expecting. I made it to the shore in less than a minute. I crawled out of the water, untied the rocks, and threw them away. I shoved the shoelaces in the pocket of my jacket.

This is the part of the story where you might expect me to

get on my knees and thank God for allowing me to live. The part where I laugh at myself for the silliness of my plan. The part where I hit rock bottom, and finally start to find my way out. That's not what happened, though.

I stood there a few seconds, staring at the Falls, the sign of my failure. *You can't even kill yourself right.* I started to creep home. The weather was still chilly and damp. So was I, inside and out. *That plan was so stupid. It never would have worked.*

I know.

And you didn't even want it to work the moment you started.

I know.

I wasn't happy to be alive—I was miserable because I was a failure. I made my way home dripping wet, jeans chafing my legs, unlaced shoes flopping on and off. As I entered the house through the back door, I heard one of my mother's piano students playing "The Wigwam Song." It was always that song. I hated that song.

I snuck upstairs to my bedroom without anyone noticing. I took off my wet clothes and threw them in the laundry basket. I put on a bathrobe and walked slowly to the bathroom. I got in the shower, wanting to wash off the filth that clung to me. The water steamed, stinging my skin. The outside of my body was warm and clean, but I felt so cold in my bones, so trapped in this cold cave I'd never escape. I shivered as warm tears mingled with hot water. I had failed. In every possible way, I had failed.

CHAPTER 7
THE POEM IN MY WALLET

AGE 17 YEARS AND 3 MONTHS

The intensity of the worries about Lily and Cathy faded fairly quickly. The feelings that led me to the Falls stayed with me. Feelings of failure clung to me like those soaked jeans. Whenever I made a mistake, the Dark Voice kept talking to me in words like these:

> *You have hurt someone. You should have known better. If you're so smart, then why do you do this? If you're such a Christian, then why do you act this way? And don't you dare think that you can grow or change. You've been here so many times. Sure, you can be nice and kind for a few hours, maybe a day, but before long, we're back here again in the same place. The very same place. You don't change. You can't change. Ever. This is who you are forever.*

I should be clear that this was a truly absurd overreaction. The mistakes I'm talking about here are things like this:

- Making a joke about someone's hair
- Making fun of someone behind their back
- Talking back to my parents
- Playing video games when I knew I should be reading
- Telling my sister that my need to use the phone was more important than hers
- Blowing my nose too loudly so it bothered someone
- Anything—absolutely anything—that made me feel like someone was upset with me or annoyed with me

In reality, I was not a bully, an abuser, or a murderer. I was not a terrible person. I was a kid who was nice sometimes and thoughtless and inconsiderate at other times. I didn't deserve the kind of lashing the Dark Voice gave me. And yet that's how I saw myself in the fun-house mirror of depression.

I didn't see myself like that all the time, but on and off consistently. About a year after my suicide attempt at the Falls, I wrote a poem that I carried in my wallet to make sure I never forgot.

> What is the point of living
> If your life is spent
> Ruining the lives of others?
> Would it not be a
> Far, far better thing
> If you were dead?
> Oh, some may feel pain at the loss

But would that pain not pale in comparison
To the pain your continued life
Would continue to inflict
On still others?
Perhaps the answer is to change
But change is not always possible
We cannot change our very being
We are what we are.
But in those brief moments of enlightenment
When we are permitted to see ourselves
We are not always satisfied.
If we realize that the change cannot come
Because the brief moments are so brief
And the enlightenment never lasts
Never lasts long enough to change,
When these moments occur
Should we not take immediate action
Before the enlightenment is gone?
Change may be better than death
But is not death better than stagnation?

-

This poem exemplifies a moment when I felt *peccator* (sinner) but not *iustus* (saint), as I described in the introduction. It's like I was trying to rewrite parts of Psalm 51, lines like "For I know my transgressions, and my sin is ever before me" (v.3) and "Indeed, I was born guilty, a sinner when my mother conceived me" (v. 5). David is said to have written this Psalm after his adulterous and murderous affair with Bathsheba. But these proclamations of guilt are not the point of the Psalm—the point is that the Psalmist asked God for forgiveness and trusted that God would provide it.

"Create in me a clean heart, O God, and put a new and right spirit within me. Do not cast me away from your presence, and do not take your holy spirit from me" (vv. 10-11). My depression made it so hard for me to believe that forgiveness was real, and so hard to believe it was for me, that I didn't even ask for it. I tried to cast myself away from God's presence.

CHAPTER 8
FRESHMAN POETRY

AGE 17 YEARS AND 8 MONTHS

My first semester at college was intense with so many new experiences. No parental oversight, inspiring classes, new friends, and exploration with alcohol and marijuana. I thought this would be a new beginning for me, and it was. But the more friends I made, the more new things I tried, the more excitement I found, the lonelier I felt. This was normal, of course. Part of adolescence is loneliness, the feeling that nobody understands you.

But my depression added to my loneliness. The Dark Voice was still with me every step in college, growing and learning and maturing along with me. These were his new words: *you feel this way because you deserve pain.* To my confused brain, my loneliness was there because I had created it, and I deserved nothing less. I couldn't see any hope within it. By this point, I had also lost my faith in God (more on that in the next chapter), so I couldn't rely on that.

I wrote a lot of poetry that first semester, and loneliness was certainly a theme. Here are a few of my poems.

MY PATH
I amble down a lonesome path
Through a forest green
The path, the trees, their roots and leaves
Are all that can be seen
I like to wander down my path
Slowly and all alone
No friend to see for miles around
That feeling chills my bones
Although this route is one I chose
And I can still turn home
I fear I shan't escape its thorn
This path will bear my tomb
When or why or how I chose
This road I can't recall
I know the child that chose my path
Still lies deep behind my wall
This path, it is a part of me
My blood flows through its stones
And it must be my destiny
To walk my path alone

A TRAPPED CHILD

The sky burns
But I do not feel it
The earth melts
But I stay frozen
The dawn destroys the never-ending night
But I am still enveloped in darkness
I cry out for something
Or someone
But no one hears my screams
They cannot hear me
I am trapped
Trapped in a cage I built many years ago
I feel happy
But I cannot feel
I feel angry
But I cannot feel
I feel sad
And I can be glimpsed
I feel frightened
And I can be seen
I feel the throes of depression
And that is where I reside
I scream for more
But I block you all out
None may see me as I really am
The world is hot and harsh
I could not survive in it
I need a façade

A barrier to protect me from the sun
I provide that shell
And keep me safe
So safe I cannot move
I cannot breathe
I am slowly suffocating
Under my own love

Psalm 88 is a psalm of lament and evokes images similar to those of my poem:

"You have put me in the depths of the Pit, in the regions dark and deep. Your wrath lies heavy upon me, and you overwhelm me with all your waves. I am shut in so that I cannot escape; my eye grows dim through sorrow" (Psalms 88:6–9).

Almost a third of the book of Psalms are lament psalms, which are cries to God to see what pain the author is enduring and pleas for God to come to the rescue. They remind us that suffering is real, even for the faithful. Living with pain, whether physical or emotional or spiritual, is not a sign of God's abandonment. Rather, it is a call for sufferers to cry out honestly and put their trust in God. While my poem is certainly not in the same poetic league as the Psalms, it has a similar intent—honestly calling out my pain, crying for help. What I wasn't able to do at that point was make that cry explicitly to God.

CHAPTER 9
TURN ON, TUNE IN, DEVOUT

AGE 17 YEARS AND 10 MONTHS

When I started college, my faith in God was gone. It had dissolved sometime during my senior year in high school. The reason for this was rather simple: it occurred to me that I had never really decided to be Lutheran. I had never really decided to believe in Christ or in God at all. I realized that the reason I believed as I did was because I was brought up that way from early childhood. I was raised by a pastor and a church organist, so faith was just part of the air in the house. It was a kind of benign brainwashing. When I realized this, I wasn't angry at the church or at my parents. I wasn't upset, but I did feel disoriented and off-balance. I realized that the faith I had wasn't my own—it was theirs. I needed to figure it out for myself. I needed to learn who I was and find my own way.

So I decided to explore other faiths. Now, by "explore other faiths," I mean I read about half a dozen books—stuff about Native American religion and stuff like *Zen and the Art of Motorcycle Maintenance*. I started to think Buddhism sounded interesting. But I had trouble with all of this: I felt like the bottom had dropped out of my belief system, and I had no idea how to build it up again without a floor. I can remember writing this with watercolor paint on the wall in my bedroom: "You can't look for answers in a book when one of your questions is whether or not to believe the book."

During the summer between high school and college, I started to think that I'd never figure out what I believed. How could I know if I really believed something? What if it was just a phase? And why would I even want to believe something just for its own sake? I thought I was so deep.

When I arrived at college, my search for truth became both more intense and less important. I started caring less about religion and faith, and I started caring more about who on earth I was. I couldn't figure myself out. I couldn't find the foundation, the floor, the rock upon which to build.

Then one night, my faith returned home.

I sat there in Amanda's dorm room, cross-legged on the floor across from her. I was excited. I'd never done this before. Her roommate walked in. Amanda smiled at her. I looked over and stuck my tongue out, showing her the tab slowly dissolving there. "Ah," the roommate said. "Have fun!"

Amanda and I got up, waved in a friendly way, and walked out into the night, leaving her roommate behind. "Come on," Amanda said, taking my hand.

We wandered across campus to Ryan's dorm; he and Amanda went to the same college, and I was visiting them both for the weekend. We went in and told him about the lysergic acid flowing through our veins, and he got excited. Not that he would ever try such things. But he was a showman, and he tried to entertain us. He succeeded. Our eyes goggled as he pretended to have magical powers. He thought we were so far gone that we believed in his magic. We weren't, but we were far enough gone to find it endlessly amusing to play along.

Then the fire alarm went off—a blaring, screaming, screeching, mind-tearing sound. It sounded like a call to arms, like some security force was being summoned to contain and eliminate a threat. I felt as though I were the threat—an interloper, a criminal, a druggie—and I had to get out of there. I started shaking. Amanda grabbed my hand and said, "Come on." We left our magical friend behind. As we dashed away from campus, Amanda said, "I don't know about you, but that alarm really made me paranoid."

We walked the streets of that college town, talking and walking and talking and walking. We didn't get tired. I guess you can't get tired when you're tripping on acid. Or at least you can't sleep. Either way, I had no desire to rest. I just wanted to keep talking, keep listening, keep exploring, and keep learning. It was late, way past midnight. I think I remember where we ended up.

I have a bifurcated memory of a place at which we stopped to talk about something very serious. On one level, I'm sure that it was the basement of Amanda's dorm, a large common room with tables, chairs, and couches. But on another level, I have a vivid memory that we were in a church basement, surrounded by chalkboards, fading "Books of the Bible" posters, and boxes of old nursery toys. I think somehow both of these memories are true. The conversation that was about to begin would link the two together in my mind. Either way, we were alone, and we kept talking.

I don't know how LSD affects brain chemistry, but I know how it felt to me that night. I felt the neurons and synapses in my brain pulsing. I could see the pathways that had been dug in my brain over seventeen years, the mental trails I'd hiked many times over. I felt these pathways become fuzzy. I felt the connections between neurons loosen. And I felt that this was a moment when I could rearrange them, when I could become something different. Something new. I listened to Amanda talking about Christ. She was telling me about God—how important God always was to her, how important God used to be to me, and how much God still loves me. She reminded me of our shared youth experiences, including the Lutheran youth events that she, Ryan, and I used to attend.

The room around me shifted from dorm common room to church basement, from beer pong to shuffleboard, and back and forth again. It felt like the neurons in my brain were firing anew in an old direction, finding the faith I'd once had and reigniting it. I was unearthing the baptismal covenant and finding it still dripping with life; I was rediscovering the hope and peace I'd forgotten about. As a rainbow of God-colored sparks cascaded through my brain, it occurred to me that I'd been trying to *think* my way back into faith for the past year. But faith is something that exists at a level beneath, or behind, thought. As I smiled with the recognition that God loved me, it felt as though my brain had rebooted, and I believed again. That night, during my one and only acid trip, my faith came back.

PART TWO
DELIVER US FROM EVIL

CHAPTER 10
FURTHER FROM FINE

AGE 17 YEARS, 10 MONTHS, AND 23 DAYS

One day in November, I was playing *Doom* on my roommate's computer while listening to Pink Floyd when the phone rang. I paused the game and answered the phone. It was my dear old friend Ryan. He said, "Listen. My drama class is taking a field trip to see a play tomorrow afternoon, and I just realized that the theater is like a mile from you. I was wondering if you might be available for coffee afterward?"

I happily agreed, and then I went back to destroying imps and demons with my shotgun.

The next night, Ryan picked me up at my dorm, and we drove to a diner. And that night, I did something I never thought possible—I gave Ryan the Mike Treatment.

I'd never done it to a friend before, only girlfriends. But I did it to Ryan, my oldest friend who had known me since kindergarten. We were sitting in the diner, talking normally, and I felt a dark cloud come over my mind.

He was talking about music. "Did you know that they're playing a Beatles marathon all weekend on WPNO? Every song in alphabetical order. I'm planning on sitting next to my radio and recording all of it on tapes."

I didn't say anything. I was looking down into my coffee.

The song playing in the diner changed to "Closer to Fine." Ryan looked up and said, "Oh, I love the Indigo Girls." He sang along.

I kept looking down.

He stopped singing and said, "What's wrong?"

I looked up at him and said, "Nothing. I just don't know why you're hanging around with me. You've known me for so long that you should know better by now."

He tilted his head. "Mike, what are you talking about? You're one of my best friends!"

I looked down again and shook my head. "No. No, I'm not. I'm nobody's friend. You're one of the kindest people I've ever known, and I know you just want to be nice to people, but you don't have to be nice to me anymore. You have your friends at school. You have Amanda there. Just be with them. Don't waste your time coming to see me anymore."

"Whoa, whoa, hold on. Does this have something to do with Amanda? Did something happen between you two when you came to see us?"

The waitress walked over and refilled both of our cups. "Anything else I can get you boys?"

Ryan smiled at her and responded, "No thanks. I think we're good." He looked back at me.

"This has nothing to do with Amanda. This is about me. I'm useless. I'm a terrible friend. Look, you'd be better off without me," I said.

"I would never be better off without you. I love you. You are funny. You're smart. I love talking with you," Ryan said.

"You're just fooling yourself. Or I've fooled you. I'm not loyal at all. All I ever do is hurt people. Remember when I came to visit a few weeks ago? I barely spent any time with you—Amanda and I were too busy doing other things. What kind of friend does that?"

"Yeah, I was kind of upset about that. But I got over it. Hey, she's your friend too. That's why I wanted to make sure to see you tonight."

I shook my head. "Then let tonight be the end. Say goodbye to me and don't look back. You're a good person, a good friend. You don't deserve a friend like me. You should be spending time with people who are worth it. I'm sorry you felt you had to waste your time with me tonight. It doesn't matter."

He shook his head and said, "Don't do this to me. Look, you told me you had a religious experience with Amanda. You found God again. You know that's a miracle. And you know that God made a miracle in you. Don't make the miracle of your existence smaller through your doubts and fears. If you trust me for anything I say or do in the time you know me, trust me on this—you matter a lot."

I sipped some coffee and said, "I'm sorry. You're one of the smartest people I know. But you somehow missed something. You just don't know the real me."

He said, "I've known you for twelve years! You're a good person."

I looked him right in the eye and said with quiet fury, "No. I'm not. I'm not good at all. You just don't understand. You're a good person. That's why you have always treated me so well. But you don't deserve to spend your pity on me. I'm sorry. I'm just so sorry."

He grabbed a napkin and blew his nose. "Look, why don't I take you back to your dorm," he said. He reached into his pocket to get his wallet out. "We'll talk about this another day. But let me tell you something: you are my friend, and I am not going to just walk out on you." He stood up and put a few dollars on the table for a tip. "Come on, let's go." He walked over to the register and paid for our coffees and desserts.

As we drove, I apologized. I said that I didn't know what came over me. I said that I was all right, and I was just tired. I would be okay in the morning. He could forget about everything I said.

When we arrived back on campus, I thanked him for the coffee and apologized again.

"Are you sure you're all right?" he said

I nodded.

"Okay," he said. "I'll give you a call next week sometime, okay?" I nodded again.

I got out of the car, and he drove off. I could see him crying as he drove, and I realized what I'd done.

I knew this guilty feeling. I'd experienced it every time I did this to Robin, to Melissa, to each of my past girlfriends. But this was different. This was more. If I did this to Ryan, then I had gone beyond the pale. I had hit rock bottom and crossed the Rubicon. There was no going back from this. If I could do this, there was no limit to what I would do. And something needed to be done.

CHAPTER 11
THE FINAL CUT (PART TWO)

AGE 17 YEARS, 10 MONTHS, AND 26 DAYS

The entire semester had been such a crazy, emotional time for me. My whole identity was in flux. I didn't know who I was or who I wanted to be. Despite the recent renaissance of my faith, I felt great despair. Not all the time—I certainly had many happy moments, some good days—but the overall tenor of my first semester was hyperactive confusion. My emotions were always on a razor's edge. I remember smoking a lot of unfiltered Lucky Strikes.

The night I gave the Mike Treatment to Ryan, something cracked. That night, I gave in to the Dark Voice and finally admitted that he was right all along, that I was indeed worthless. It would in fact be better if I were not here. The world would be better off without me. And when I did that, he went silent. He left me alone. I sat on that cracked feeling for a few days. It was cold like concrete on a winter day. But it was quiet in my head. And the pain was gone. It had always hurt so much to wonder if I were worthless. Now I felt like there was no wondering anymore; it was a certainty.

I felt a sense of calm. Peace. Direction. The feeling was cold and raw, but calm. It was only a matter of time. I just needed to work this out. Calmly, patiently, slowly.

During my classes, I made notes about methods in the margins of my notebooks. A gun wasn't an option because I wouldn't even know where to get one. While eating in the cafeteria, I thought about poison. What foods could I combine? Or was there a way to break into the chemistry lab and steal chemicals or to break into the health center and steal medicine? I didn't know enough about either field to know what to get. And I was no burglar, so I'd probably get caught, and what would happen then? I'd get kicked out of college and lose any chance of doing this gracefully. I wanted to *stop* upsetting people, not upset people even more with my last act. I wondered why suicide had to be so difficult. *Why can't we just will ourselves to die?* I thought. *Why does it take so much effort to just stop living?*

Then, as I was walking around campus, I saw a tall tree with long horizontal branches. It beckoned to me. *That's it.* That would work. All I needed was a noose. But I wouldn't do it here on campus because I would get caught way too easily. It had to be somewhere more secluded where I could do it without being disturbed.

Later that day, I walked down the hill to a park a few blocks off campus. I walked around, examining the trees. It had to be the right height, the right strength, the right hiddenness. This park wasn't exactly wooded, but there were a few spots here and there with groups of trees. I found a patch of mature hemlocks and walked in. Their branches were full and hung low to the ground, so there was enough seclusion. I looked at each of the branches and found one that looked easily climbable. I grabbed hold of a low limb and climbed up. I was standing on a good solid branch about ten feet off the ground, and I could reach up to another one that was just as strong. This would do. I was done looking. This was it.

I stood there on that branch, holding onto the one above, the one that would soon hold a noose. *I will stand here again*, I thought. *And I will take my last breath here.* I felt tears well up in the corners of my eyes, but they did not fall. I stared into the distance, seeing the sun's light, low in the west, trying to shine through gray clouds. I shivered. *This is right*, I told myself. And I believed it. I was ready for this. It was long overdue. I just needed to keep control. Just tamp down any nagging feelings of changing my mind just long enough to do it.

I climbed back down. It had to be soon. I couldn't wait long. I went home to think about what I'd need. I needed to think of everything.

The next night, I popped the soundtrack to *Godspell* into my Walkman and shoved it in the pocket of my jacket. I had loved that soundtrack since early childhood when I would dance to my parents' record of it. Over the years, along with *Jesus Christ Superstar*, it became a soundtrack to my faith. I knew every song on *Godspell* in great detail—the exact sound of the shofar at the beginning of "Prepare Ye," the way the lead and background singers didn't sing the same words in "By My Side," and the order in which the instruments were added in "We Beseech Thee." I knew these songs, and I knew what they meant for me—the salvation story and the story of God's love for the world through the life of Jesus Christ.

I had brought these cassettes with me to college even though my faith had been so confused. And now that my faith was back, I thought that *Godspell* would be perfect. I needed courage. I believed that God provided courage to the faithful, and I thought that listening to *Godspell* would help me remember that. I thought that it would distract me from the voices telling me to stop—the voices of fear and the survival instinct—and instead allow me to listen to the voice of God, the voice that I thought wanted me to go through with this. I believed that God wanted this, or at the very least, that God understood that this was better than the alternative: if I couldn't change, and I knew I couldn't, then this was the best alternative. God would help. I just needed to pray. I put the headphones over my ears and walked out of my dorm into the night.

With hippie hymns playing in my ears, I retraced my steps from the day before to the park. I prayed for courage as I walked. I watched the cars drive by, wondering if the drivers would care about what was going to happen if they knew. I watched as a few bats flew overhead, wondering if they'd care. I crossed the street and went straight to the hemlock I'd chosen. Standing there at night, I was pleased to notice that I couldn't see the road, so it would stand to reason that no one could see me. I stood there, turned off the Walkman, and leaned against the tree. "Give me strength. I know you want me to do this. This is the right choice. Give me strength." I balled my fists. I breathed slowly. I turned the tape back on and climbed the tree.

I reached the limb I had stood on the day before and reached up to grab the limb above. I removed the bungee cord that I was wearing as a belt and wrapped it around my neck. I reached up to wind it around the branch above me. I was crying. My survival instinct was kicking in, and a big part of me did not want to do this. But another part was so sure that I had to do it. I was not going to make the same mistake I had made at the Falls. Once I jumped, there would be no going back. Just a snap, and that would be the end. I turned the volume up, and heard these old, old words from "O Bless the Lord, My Soul" by James Montgomery:

> He will not always chide
> He will with patience wait
> His wrath is ever slow to rise
> And ready to abate
> Oh bless the Lord my soul!

Yes. Here we go. I am going to do this. I have to do this. This is right. This is right. God, God, O GOD, give me the strength to do this! The tears flowed freely now,
 . . . and . . .
 . . . and I saw a light in the distance.

Near the horizon, a bright light suddenly shone. It was a beacon, a lighthouse shining through the darkness. It was probably just a streetlight popping on or someone's garage door opening, but all I saw was a light. Nothing more. Just a flash of brightness amid the dark.

To me in that moment, it was a sign, and the surest sign I'd ever seen. It was the Star of Bethlehem shining in the sky, the star that once led the magi to the Christ child. It was the Light that shines in the darkness, and the darkness cannot overcome it. It was the Light of the World not hidden under a bushel but out in the open for all to see. It was a sign from God, from the Lord, my Light, and my Salvation.

It was a message from God saying, "No." I could almost hear the voice of God saying to me, "NO. DO NOT DO THIS. CLIMB BACK DOWN."

I turned off the Walkman. My tears started flowing more freely. I felt their warmth on my face, and I felt released. I sat down on the limb of the tree, leaning against the trunk. I felt sap all over the leg of my jeans, but I didn't care. I could feel its tackiness. I could feel! The branch beneath me felt sturdy and hard. The air on my face felt chilly and damp. The cord still wrapped around my neck felt taut, and I quickly pulled it off and dropped it on the ground. I was here. I was breathing, and I was going to keep going. God had spoken to me. God had sent me a sign. I felt seen. I felt real. I felt present.

I noticed I still had the headphones on, and I remembered that I had been hoping for strength from God through the songs. I gingerly pressed play again on the Walkman, curious what I might hear. I heard this (again from "O Bless the Lord, My Soul"):

> He pardons all thy sins
> Prolongs thy feeble breath
> He healeth thine infirmities
> And ransoms thee from death

I hit stop again, took off the headphones, and hung them around my neck. I climbed back down the tree and wiped my tears.

I walked back to my dorm, listening to the sounds around me—a dog barked, a few cars drove by, a distant siren wailed. I was hearing the sounds of real life all around me. I was part of it all.

I entered my dorm room. My roommate was already asleep. I decided that I would think about what to do next tomorrow. I quietly crawled into bed and fell asleep quickly.

CHAPTER 12
IT WASN'T MONO

AGE 17 YEARS, 10 MONTHS, AND 30 DAYS

Blech. I felt blech and blah. I had a cold—a bad one—with a sore throat, runny nose, and fuzziness in the head. I wondered if it was something worse. Bronchitis, maybe? People were saying that mono was going around. Could that be it? I didn't like this feeling, and I wanted it to stop. Sounds silly since I'd just tried to kill myself a few days earlier, and now I wanted relief from a bad cold? I guess I just wanted the pain to stop. If I were home, I would have asked my mother to take me to the doctor. At college, I had the health center to rely on.

It was about 3:00 p.m. My last class had just ended, and I coughed myself over to the student health center. A nurse in the main room welcomed me. She was friendly with a warm smile. I remembered her from when I'd sprained my arm the month before. She was so kind then. I told her my symptoms, and she nodded sympathetically. She led me into an examination room where I sat on the table. She looked in my ears, had me say "ah," and checked my neck for any swelling. After a while, she said, "I don't see anything physically wrong. Have you been under any stress lately?"

See, here's the thing. I trusted this nurse—I always trusted doctors and nurses. And I always thought that they couldn't do their job unless they had all the information. I never told white lies to a doctor to make myself look better. If I did that, how could they help me properly? So I figured there was nothing to do but tell the truth.

What should I say? That I was depressed? Maybe. But I was always depressed. Tell her that I was more depressed than usual? Was I though? I thought I had been feeling better since seeing the light. Hadn't I? Or maybe I hadn't. The light was fading. I wasn't sure if I'd done the right thing by stopping myself. I thought that maybe I should just say, "Yes, I've been under stress." The one thing I should definitely not say was, "Well, I did try to kill myself a few days ago." So what did I say?

"Well, I did try to kill myself a few days ago."

That was the first time I'd mentioned it to anyone. I hadn't mentioned it to my roommate. I hadn't mentioned it to Ryan or Amanda. Nobody knew about my suicide attempt except me and that tree, and now this one nurse who stood there staring at me. For a few seconds, the only movement she made was her quivering lip. Then she said, "Stay here a minute. I'll be right back."

As I sat there alone, I wondered what had just happened. Why had I said that? I had no concept of the power in the words I'd just spoken, but I was going to learn. With that one sentence, I created the next two weeks. Perhaps the next twenty years.

The Bible tells us that God created the whole of creation with words. Looking back now, I guess I can see how that's possible. As I sat there alone for five minutes, I started to worry. What was she doing? What was she getting? To whom was she talking?

She came back and asked me to follow her. She led me to the other end of the building, which was the counseling center, and we entered the office of one of the counselors. The room was full of dark wooden furniture, stacks of paper, and books on every flat surface. The counselor thanked the nurse as she left. He looked at me and said, "Hi there. Have a seat."

I sat on a maroon chair opposite his desk. It looked like leather to me, but I wasn't sure. It looked like it was supposed to be expensive and luxurious, but I didn't like it at all. I felt like it would either swallow me whole or spit me out on the floor.

The counselor sat behind his desk and asked, "How are you doing, Michael?" He had broad shoulders and a bit of a gut, a receding hairline, and a thick mustache. He spoke in a deep voice, which intimidated me.

"I'm okay."

"I understand you attempted suicide a few days ago."

I swallowed and said, "Not quite. I stopped myself before I went through with it."

"Why did you stop yourself?" he asked.

I did not trust this guy, and I didn't know what was happening here. As willing as I'd been to tell the nurse my life story, I suddenly found myself taciturn.

"I guess I just changed my mind."

He played with a pencil, bouncing it off his desk without taking his eyes off me. "Do you know about depression, Michael?"

Oh, for crying out loud. Here we go, I thought. *It's the Care Team all over again.* My mind started to drift. I kept enough of my attention on the counselor that I could answer his questions, which seemed so trite and banal to me: "How are your grades? What's your home life like? What makes Michael tick?" With the rest of my attention, I worked on how I could get out of this. Mom wasn't going to come and save me like she did in junior high school. I did not want to talk with this guy any longer. How could I convince him that I was fine now? What would happen if I just got up and left? Was there any way I could still get some medicine for my cold?

I finally just said, "I'm sorry, but it's getting late. I appreciate your concern, but I'm doing much better than I was on Sunday night. Can I go now?"

"No," he said. "I'm afraid you can't. It's our policy that you can't leave this building until you are picked up by your parents. You'll have to leave campus until you have a doctor's note saying that you're no longer a danger to yourself." He handed me a phone and invited me to call my parents.

I was shocked and appalled. This was surreal. This was the Care Team on crack. I felt the walls closing in on me. My heart raced. My mind crashed. I didn't need a doctor's note for any such thing. I was just trying to be honest with the nurse, to get the most appropriate care for my cold.

I muttered something under my breath. The counselor misheard me and said, "Motherfucker? Yeah, you can call me motherfucker. That's fine."

I corrected him. "That's not what I said. I said, 'What the hell?'" I glared at him and picked up the phone. I dialed, and my mother answered. "Hi, Mom. It's me. I'm so sorry, but can you come and pick me up? I'm in the counseling center, and they won't let me leave unless you get me. I tried to kill myself a few days ago."

She started to cry and promised to be there right away. And then I sat in that ridiculous red chair in that wooden office for another hour. The counselor stayed quiet, perhaps waiting for me to talk first. I didn't say a word. I sat in the chair looking around at the paintings and diplomas on the walls. Inside, I was twisted up in knots. I felt like everything was out of my control. I couldn't walk out of there. My stomach churned, and my head hurt. I didn't want any of this—this wasn't the kind of help I ever wanted. I felt under attack.

An hour later, my mother arrived. She hugged me, and then she spoke with the counselor for a few minutes. I just sat there staring at the wall, not wanting to hear any of it. We drove over to my dorm where I gathered some clothes and things and shoved them in a duffel bag. My roommate wasn't there, so I left him a note saying that I had to go home suddenly, and that I'd be back soon. After I finished the note, I said to Mom, "I need to let my professors know too."

She said, "The counselor said he would take care of that."

I shook my head. "I don't trust him. I'd like to go and see if my advisor is in his office. Is that all right?"

She agreed and we walked over to the building where his office was. Dr. Neland was indeed there, packing up his briefcase. He said, "Michael, how are you?"

I gave him the short version. "Actually, not great. I tried to kill myself a few days ago, and now the counseling center is sending me home until I have a note saying I can safely come back."

He put his briefcase down and furrowed his brow. "I'm so sorry," he said. "What can I do?"

"I was hoping you'd let my other professors know," I said.

"Absolutely." He turned to my mother. "I'm sorry, I don't know if we've met."

I apologized and introduced them.

Dr. Neland turned back to me and said, "I'll take care of everything with the administration and your professors. Don't give that another thought. Just get better and come back when you're ready." He reached out and gave me a hug. I could tell this was affecting him deeply.

As my mother and I walked out toward the car, I thought about the reactions both Dr. Neland and the counselor had to my words. Why was everyone taking this so seriously? Why was this such a big deal to everyone? Why did they care if I lived or died? I just wanted this to end. I didn't want to go back home with my mother. I didn't want to see some doctor about this. I just wanted to go back to my regular life. I just wanted to go back and play video games on my roommate's computer. It felt like I was being taken away in handcuffs or a straitjacket because I'd stopped myself from being taken away on a funeral bier. It wasn't fair.

CHAPTER 13
DAYS OF HOPE

AGE 17 YEARS, 11 MONTHS

"Holy cats! You can't bring a billy club to a mental hospital!" I couldn't believe those words came out of my mouth. For a lot of reasons. I looked around to make sure nobody else had heard.

Ryan closed his jacket so I could no longer see the offending weapon he was hiding there. "Hey," he said. "I don't know this city well, and I didn't know what we might encounter. Don't worry, I'm not going to sell it to anyone here or anything. Wait— how much do you think I could get?" He smiled a huge grin. We both laughed.

The two of us were sitting on my bed at St. James Hospital. It was visiting hours, and he had driven all the way up here to see me. It was so wonderful to see him. I could almost convince myself it was old times—Ryan and I laughing together and picking on each other. But of course it wasn't the same. We weren't on the same level; I was the patient, and he was the visitor. I was the broken one, and he was here to see me in my brokenness. It felt good to know he cared, but at the same time, I felt fragile, cracked, and weak. I suppose I was all of those things, but it wasn't pleasant to acknowledge that.

"How are you, Mike?" he said. "I mean, really. How are you really?" He looked at me intently.

"Better. I'm getting better."

"I'm glad to hear it. Really, I am," he said. He looked around and said, "You know, this really isn't all that different from a dorm room. I thought it would be more like a hospital."

He was right. It was a roomy space, with two beds, two dressers, two desks, and a closet. The floor had green carpet, and the walls were a pale blue. The windows, however, were covered in metal grating, just in case you had suicidal thoughts.

I nodded. "It's a lot better than my first night here, I'll tell you that!"

"What was that like? Tell me the story."

And so I told him.

It was dark by the time my mother and I arrived home from college. My father and my sister were waiting in the living room for us. At first, there was an astringent silence. There was grief in the air. Eventually, my father said, "I called a counselor I used to work with. I asked her what we should do when you got here. She said that we should take you to St. James Hospital tonight."

"Tonight?" I replied. "It's late. Can't we try to go tomorrow?"

My father shook his head. "She was very clear on that. Tonight."

I closed my eyes and said, "Fine. Maybe we can get this taken care of tonight, and you can drive me back to school tomorrow."

Dad said, "Michael, this is for real. You need to get help. I don't think you're going back tomorrow."

I sighed. "Okay. My stuff is still in Mom's car."

I hugged my sister, who stayed behind as my parents drove me to the hospital about twenty miles away. It was a forbidding building on a side street, four stories of white walls with bars on the windows. Once we arrived, I followed my parents in.

They were expecting me there; my father had called ahead. I met with an intake counselor who asked me the same questions the college counselor had asked, the same questions the Care Team had asked all those years ago. I was so tired of all these questions, and so tired of trying to convince people I was fine. So tired.

"I think you should admit yourself to the hospital," the intake counselor suggested to me after listening to those same answers.

"But I'm fine," I said. "I wasn't fine a few days ago, but I'm fine now."

"I understand that. But I still think it would be the best choice to admit yourself tonight," he said.

I looked at my parents. They were both fighting back tears. My father said, "Michael, it's probably for the best."

I signed the papers. I found out a few days later that they would have sought a court order to have me committed had I refused. They brought me up to the adult ward. I was trembling as an aide showed me around: the common room, the payphones, the private therapy rooms, the group therapy rooms, and the bedrooms. "Only you won't be sleeping here tonight," she said. "We're full right now, so you'll be taken out at bedtime to sleep in another ward. Other than that, you'll be in here all day. Until we take you off suicide watch, you'll be eating your meals up here, and you won't be able to go on field trips with the others."

My dad gave me a credit card. He said, "Use this for phone calls. Call anybody you like, as much as you like. Don't worry about the bill." My parents hugged me, and they promised to come the next day during visiting hours. Then the door was locked. I was alone. And I was scared.

I managed to avoid most contact with the other patients when they returned from supper. I sat through a group therapy session and said as little as I could. I just clung to my duffel bag, wishing it was all a dream. Finally I was told it was bedtime, and I was led, along with a middle-aged man, out the locked door, down the elevator, and into another locked ward. There he and I slept in a room with two other men, one of whom snored like a feral jackhammer. Between the nasally impaired beast and my own fear of what lay ahead the next day, I got almost no sleep at all.

"Sheesh," Ryan said. "It sounds like a prison." He glanced out into the hall, as though worried that a guard might pass by. The only person out there was one of my fellow patients, pacing back and forth. Ryan pointed to her and said quietly, "Hey, is she all right?"

I looked out and nodded. "Yeah, that's Janet. She paces a lot, says it's for exercise."

"How long have you been here now? A week?" he asked.

"Today's the eighth day."

"I'm sorry I couldn't come sooner," he said. "I was trying to convince Amanda, but . . ." He trailed off and looked away.

"It's okay," I said. "My parents have been here every day, and I've talked to so many people on the phone. I'm shocked at how upset people are, to be honest."

"How can that surprise you?"

"I guess I just didn't think I mattered that much. I certainly don't matter to Amanda, do I?"

Ryan shook his head. "That's not it at all."

"She won't even talk to me on the phone. Whenever I try to call her, she just hangs up."

He was still looking down at the bed, running his hand on the scratchy quilt. "I know. She's angry. Really angry. She cares about you so much; don't you get it? That's why she's angry." He looked up at me. "That's why she's not here today. She is so mad at you for . . . well, for this . . . that she doesn't even want to see you right now."

A voice came over the loudspeaker in the hall. "Dinner is in five minutes. Everyone to the elevators in five minutes."

"I guess I have to go," Ryan said.

"Actually you don't. Visitors are allowed to come to the cafeteria with us. Would you like to stay another hour? The food's actually not bad."

We sat in the cafeteria at a table by ourselves. It was noisy in there, as most of the patients were talking and laughing with each other. The room was large with about twenty round wooden tables and four chairs around each. The cafeteria was on the ground floor. There were lots of windows looking out onto a courtyard, but each one was barred, just like upstairs. Dinner was hamburgers that night.

"You know, this isn't that bad," Ryan said.

"I told you!"

"So," Ryan said, wiping ketchup from his lip, "I'm a little surprised by something." He raised his arm and gestured toward all the people in the room. Quietly he revealed, "Everybody here seems normal."

"I know! I was really surprised by that too. There's only one Jesus here."

Ryan spit out a little of his soda. "What?"

I turned and subtly pointed toward a disheveled man at another table. "Guy in the red shirt? Thinks he's Jesus. But other than him, we're all just regular people dealing with depression or bipolar disorder or things like that. Hey, do you see her over there in the blue?"

"With the black hair?" he asked. "She's beautiful."

I nodded. "Isn't she? That's Jessica. She and I had an amazing conversation yesterday. Turns out she thinks she's absolutely worthless."

Ryan said, "Just like you sometimes. How can somebody that pretty think that? She could be a model."

"That's what I said to her! But then she asked me how somebody as smart as me could think they're worthless!"

Ryan looked out the window. The sun was going down, and the light was glinting off the fallen leaves all over the yard. He said, "We've all got our stuff, don't we?" He turned back to me and asked, "That thing that happened with me at the diner—was that part of this?"

I looked down. "Actually," I said, "that's what started it. I felt so guilty for what I did to you that I thought it would be better if, you know, I just wasn't here."

He shook his head. "Damn it, Mike."

I was quiet. I didn't know what to say. I wondered what was going through his head. Was he blaming himself? Was he angry at me like Amanda was? After a few seconds, he smiled and said, "You're doing great, though. You're happier than I've seen you in ages. What's helping?"

"A bunch of things. You, for one. All my friends and family who tell me how much I mean to them. Also, getting to know these people here and seeing that I'm not alone in feeling the way I do. They're like a mirror to me. And if they're okay then maybe I am too. Oh, and that courtyard outside. Just getting out there and breathing the air and crunching the leaves—I never knew how much I like autumn. And we went bowling yesterday. You have no idea how much fun that was after being cooped up in here for four days. I'm planning on going to church with them on Sunday too."

"Yeah, how's your faith doing through all this?"

"Right now, it's great. I'm learning how to trust again. In fact, I wrote a poem in one of our therapy sessions this morning. I'll show it to you before you leave, if I remember."

One of the nurses stood up and shouted, "All right, everybody! Time to get back upstairs! Group is in ten minutes!"

I stood up from the table and picked up my tray. I looked at Ryan and smiled. "I'm so glad you came. It means a lot to me." I led him to the kitchen entrance where we left our trays.

"All right. I guess I'm off," Ryan said. "I'll see you when you're out, okay? And Amanda will come around. I promise."

"That'll be great," I said.

"Wait, your poem."

"I'll mail you a copy," I promised.

He walked down the long corridor to the exit as I got in the elevator with my fellow patients. I thought about Amanda. I could not comprehend how she could be that upset. A splash of guilt came over me that I had caused her such pain. But I closed my eyes, took a deep breath, and said to myself, *Stop. It's not your fault. It means she cares about you. It's okay.* The elevator bell sounded as I opened my eyes. Jessica was standing next to me. We made eye contact and smiled. It was going to be okay. I actually believed that.

PART THREE
CHASING AFTER WIND

CHAPTER 14
TWO MORE POEMS

AGE 17-18

While I was at the hospital, I discovered Romans 8. The latter portion is an audacious proclamation that God's love for us is so strong that there is absolutely nothing that can separate us from that love: "For I am convinced that neither death, nor life, nor angels, nor rulers, nor things present, nor things to come, nor powers, nor height, nor depth, nor anything else in all creation, will be able to separate us from the love of God in Christ Jesus our Lord" (Romans 8:38–39). Reading this at the hospital convinced me that even if I was as horrible as I thought I was, that would not be enough to stop God from loving me. The poem I wrote when I was there was a song of trust in God.

A BELIEVER'S PRAYER
I have always been confused
About what you meant for me

I never knew what I should do
Or who to try to be
I struggled with your existence
As I struggled with my own
But now I know you love me
And I'll never be alone
Yet I still cannot be sure of
What you want me to do
Although you live inside me
It's a challenge serving you
So now I ask for help, O Lord
For you can do no wrong
I beg, when I go down again,
Your love may keep me strong
I know you have a plan for me
I know you know what's best
So I'll just keep on loving you
And let you do the rest

The Transfiguration of Jesus is recounted in Matthew 17, Mark 11, and Luke 9. In all these narrations, Jesus leads three of his apostles up a mountain, where he is transformed before them, and his clothes glow bright white. Visions of Moses and Elijah appear and speak with Jesus. Simon Peter, often the spokesperson for the apostles, seems to want to hold onto this vision and stay on top of the mountain forever. But it ends as quickly as it began, and Jesus leads them back down the mountain, onto the long journey toward the cross.

We have mountaintop experiences in our lives, when things seem perfect and amazing, but they don't last. We must always go back down the mountain into the ebb and flow of daily life. "A Believer's Prayer" was written on top of the mountain when I was full of life and joy and optimism in the hospital. The following poem was written in the valley that followed. Life went back to normal, and the depression came back.

TOTAL INTERNAL REFLECTION
When I was just a guilty child
I felt nothing in my soul
There was a gap within an empty void
It wasn't something that I noticed
Back then I wasn't quite in focus
Yet my solitude seemed whole
My childhood passed unnoticed
A childhood without a path
As it slowly finishes to fade away
I try to look back and laugh
So I turn my mind to face it
And feel my thoughts rewind
I'd had no idea I had all this
Garbage inside my mind
I return into my self now
And I see what this has spurned
Just a tired boy in love with his alter ego
Trying to write you a song

CHAPTER 15

STANDING OUTSIDE A BROKEN COLLEGE HOUSE WITH MY WALKMAN IN MY HAND

AGE 19-21

I was standing out on the porch again. The house I lived in for three years at college had a porch on the first floor that wrapped around one side and the back of the house. There was an old table holding a few empty beer bottles, a bicycle with one flat tire lying on the floor, and a fire escape leading up to the triple room on the third floor. About eighteen people lived in Bernheim House, most of us involved in some way in the theater program, and this porch was a communal area on nice days. But I was out there by myself again, just standing in the back corner, Walkman in hand, headphones on. From my vantage point, I stared out toward the performing arts center, the matte white wall of bricks that housed the college theater and many rehearsal spaces. As I listened to the music in my ears, I saw many people enter and exit the white wall. Sometimes they'd walk toward me, toward the house. There were friends of mine who lived here at Bernheim too.

But I usually never really noticed the people when I was on the porch like this. I was absorbed in the music, always particular music chosen specifically for these moments, like Pink Floyd's "Wish You Were Here" and "Learning to Fly." I stood there, listening, letting the sound envelop me. I wasn't really there at that moment—I was flying, soaring. I was stuck in the music, not the real world. It was safer.

There was Primitive Radio Gods' "Standing Outside a Broken Phone Booth with Money in My Hand"; the haunting melody and hypnotic rhythm section lulled me into an altered state, and the lyrics caught me and took me to places I'd never been but that felt so familiar. The song ate through my heart like an acid corroding metal. It washed over me and through me, the words and beats and notes and harmonies filling my lungs with each breath and entering every cell. My soul danced.

There was Peter Gabriel's "Digging in the Dirt," Barenaked Ladies' "What a Good Boy," U2's "One," Kansas' "Dust in the Wind," and so many more.

I stood out there on that porch so often, Walkman in hand, motionless. I had learned that music had the ability to affect my moods, and I went out there whenever I felt depressed. I didn't go out there to feel better but rather to wrap myself up in the depression. I invited the music in to enhance that feeling, to envelop and engulf me in the comfort of melancholy, to hypnotize myself into a hall of mirrors reflecting my fears and worries right back, but in a soothing 4/4 time.

In that hall of mirrors, I found the Dark Voice waiting for me. He stood there in each mirror, staring back at me with my own eyes. And from the mirror, he sang. He sang the songs that streamed through those headphones. He sang lyrics that spoke of lost love. He sang lyrics that spoke of confused identity. He sang lyrics that spoke of loneliness and death. He took lyrics that may have been about romantic love and helped me to see them as reasons why I'd always be alone. He took lyrics that may have been about hope and found a new interpretation of despair. He became a composer, a conductor, a collage artist of all the songs I continued to collect each year. In the hall of mirrors, the Dark Voice created an existential rock opera with an audience of one: me.

He whispered to me through the movements of the opera. He whispered that I was nothing but dust. He whispered that I was destined to be alone and lonely. He whispered that I was useless, that I would never find what I was looking for. His was the voice of so many singers, as well as a quiet voice between the songs, a cruel DJ who connected all the dots with studied precision. He reminded me that he made all this for me, that he was the only one who truly understood me, and that I belonged in here, in the hall of mirrors, with him. And I did. While the music played, I wanted nothing but to live inside it. I was safe, cocooned, and nested. But the song eventually ended, or the batteries ran out, or the clock led me to other responsibilities.

Those hours spent out on the porch with my Walkman felt so intense and profound in the moment, but they always left me feeling broken and tired. I look back now and see how unhealthy that really was, but at the time it felt like the most real thing in the world.

CHAPTER 16
GNAWING

AGE 20

"What do you want me to do? Do you want me to leave?" It was just past midnight, and I was standing outside her parents' house by the pool. It was a balmy summer night, and I'd come here to join Anna for some midnight swimming. I had my trunks on, and she was also dressed for swimming, but we hadn't gotten in the water yet. I'd only arrived five minutes earlier, and already we were in another fight.

Anna hissed at me, "Yes. Leave." She had a towel wrapped around her. She looked so different dressed in a swimsuit, but it was still her. Even without her usual stylish black outfit, even without the usual smoke from a clove cigarette swirling around her, it was still her—beautiful, intoxicating, filled with fire and ice.

I didn't know whether it was fire or ice that sliced through me at that moment, but I knew I didn't like it. I wasn't leaving.

I wasn't giving up on this relationship. I wasn't about to give up on her—to give up on us—just because we were fighting again. I said, "No. I'm not leaving."

She took a step closer to me, and the full moon's reflection in the pool hit her eyes. They were wide and blazing. "Leave. Now."

I refused. I was going to save us. "No," I said, matching her intensity. "I'm staying."

"Leave!"

I yelled back, "I'm not leaving!"

Her eyes changed as fear mixed in with the rage. And then I noticed I had grabbed her shoulders—not in a loving way, but in a rough, hard, violent way. She pulled away. I stared at my hands. I mumbled, "I'm leaving."

I left.

I got in my car, and I drove. The drive home normally took ten minutes, but I drove slowly and missed turns. It took me forty-five minutes to get home that night.

As I drove, my eyes were wide open, my face blank. I retreated into my head, and in there, I heard words resounding, echoing, as though in a cavern:

You are a woman-beater. You have never changed. You can never grow. You have destroyed Anna's life. You will never be forgiven for this. You will never heal from this. Your life as you know it is over. You are evil.

I knew that my relationship with Anna was over. As I drove, I realized that when she'd told me to leave, she just meant leave her house. I had thought she meant leave her life. But now I had to. I never thought it would end like this. We'd only been dating for two months, but it was so intense, so real.

Now I would have to stop dating entirely. If I was capable of what I just did to Anna, then I should never be in this kind of situation again. I would have to consider if I should even have friends anymore. I wasn't safe. I just wasn't safe. I finally got home and stared at the ceiling for hours before falling asleep.

The next day I wrote Anna a long letter. The gist of it was this: "I am so very sorry. I don't know if you can ever forgive me, but I hope that you do not believe that all men are like this. I hope that this has not traumatized you for life. You deserve better than this." I drove to her house, put the letter in her door, rang the doorbell once, and left. She called me that evening, and we talked about it. We even ended up dating for a little while longer until it all just got to be too much for both of us.

Shortly after this experience, I wrote a poem about it called "Gnawing."

> Knowledge is wonderful
> But pain is God
> All men are created even
> But I'm still odd
> I know who I am now
> But now has changed
> One fatal event
> And life is rearranged
> A flash of red, a temper that snapped
> Now I'm gnawing my foot off to escape this trap
> Without a foot, you'd think you'd still remain whole
> But right under your heel resides your soul
> A forceful election

Inside my head
And the unknown soldiers
Have been shot dead
I wish I could speak now
But who would hear
The forest tree falling
On a comatose ear
The Barenaked Ladies
Can write my songs
But there's nobody out there
To right my wrongs
The pain that I caused
Comes back a hundredfold
Before the cigarette burns out
And the wounds grow old
A flash of red, a mind that snapped
But I'm gnawing my foot off to escape this trap
Without a foot, you'd think you'd still remain whole
But right under your heel resides your soul

CHAPTER 17
ONE CRAZY EMAIL

AGE 21

After college, I began my studies at a Lutheran seminary. I quickly found that I didn't quite fit in, in several ways. First off, unlike most of my classmates, I had no desire at that time to become a pastor or a lay church worker. If pressed, I guess I thought I might leverage this degree into a doctoral program someday. But really, I just wanted to study theology.

On top of my unorthodox career plans, I found myself questioning my faith again during my first semester. When you're questioning your faith, seminary is an interesting place to be. I may not have been the only person with questions, but I was certainly one of the few willing to say, "I'm not sure if I'm Christian or not." I was also a small-town kid living in a major city. I was connected to friends and family via email but little else. It was exciting but also lonely.

One day that fall, a friend emailed me from her college in

New England. She and I were neighbors growing up, and we were certainly friends but not particularly close. From time to time we contacted each other, but this email was different. Her message was longer, more intimate, and more profound than anything she'd shared with me before. She talked to me about her love life and about her struggles with deciding to go to grad school. She told me that she was lonely and described in great detail why. She was considering if she might be happier if she were "crazy." She said she was too boring to be crazy, and that sanity made her feel dead inside—she wanted to have something alive, something to help her lose reality. And she called that "crazy."

She was reaching out for connection, I thought, something I was looking for myself. I felt that her email deserved a response in kind, and so after thinking about it all day, I wrote this:

> Crazy. I know crazy. Crazy is when you hear a song lyric, and it fits your life better than that of the author. Crazy is when you hear your name whistling in the wind. When you realize how similar we all are, and how much the human race is just one person in a billion bodies, crazy is that leftover stuff inside you that doesn't fit in with anyone else. Crazy is what you do when you look in the mirror with no one else around. All the bits in your life which you DON'T KNOW if anyone else shares, all the things that you think make you YOU, but somewhere deep-down you wonder if everyone else feels the same way. And there's no way to find out if somebody else is the same way . . . this is what drives us crazy. Embrace it and lose touch.

Ignore it and lose touch. Or ride the line of fear and excitement, the line between ignorance and embracing, and go crazy. Write an email about it and wonder if what you're saying makes any sense. Wonder if there's really anyone out there who could know what you're saying. Wonder if you'd even understand it if you read it tomorrow. Wonder if you should even mail it. Do it anyway. Either she'll think you're crazy, or she'll know you both are. Either way, if you share it, you're crazy.

All day I searched for a way to respond to your mail. I looked on Franklin Street, as I drove to church. I found only a place called Prosperity Square. I looked during church, listening to the sermon of the supply preacher. I found only a miserable attempt to connect with people gone horribly awry by an incredible lack of preaching ability mixed with an exorbitant age. I listened to the radio on the way back and heard only a strange new song by U2 about God and a strange cover of the Peter Gabriel song "In Your Eyes," which I've always held is about God. I watched my fellow seminarians watching football and found only proof that I am crazy. Crazy to be at seminary, crazy to think I could belong here, crazy to be alive. Alive to be crazy.

All I found today was loneliness. Loneliness in my friends here. Loneliness in the warmth all over outside, covering the chills who rightfully own October. Loneliness in the reading I did for my classes, the loneliness of the Bible, the story of a mythical people who may or may not have existed, who may or may not have been the chosen people of a God who may or may not have existed, and, if so, may or may not be the same God who may or may not exist today. And my own estrangement from all this.

I am lonely as well. Lonely because I saw my two best friends from college yesterday at Homecoming, and I know things will never be the same again between us. Lonely because I don't know anyone here well enough to cry in front of them, which in turn gives me the only reason I have to cry. Lonely because this place is about the dream of being a pastor, a pipe dream I don't even dream. Lonely because no one here feels the same way. Lonely because everything I know is arbitrary. Lonely because you reached out to me in a way you never have before, and in reaching back, I'm still hundreds of miles, and hundreds of mails, away.

Tomorrow I may regret mailing this, but tonight I am crazy, I suppose. This is not ridicule, and this is not fake in any way. This is me, right now. I'm showing you what craziness can be. It is black, and it is purple and blue and green. Love it if you will. Thank you for giving me an interesting day.

She never responded. I didn't know how to take that. Did I go too far? Did I say something too, well, crazy? Did I fail by making my response all about me? Or maybe she never received this email? Should I have sent it again? I wondered this for weeks. Every time I checked my email, I looked for a response from her, only to be disappointed. At first I was terrified that

I'd upset her or offended her. Over time, the terror faded, but I always wondered.

She did email me again, almost exactly a year to the day later, but never mentioned this "crazy" email. It was just a "hey, haven't heard from you in a while" kind of email. By then, I thought it was too late to ask her what happened. It's always been a mystery, and it still nags a little bit, more than twenty years later.

CHAPTER 18
NOW AND AGAIN

AGE 22

It wasn't all misery and poetry. Now and again, something wonderful happened that gave me great joy. The biggest joy of this period in my life was finally finding "her"—the one I'd always been searching for, waiting for. My soulmate, the one whom I once thought was Melissa, then Robin, then Cathy, and so forth.

This *one* was the person I learned to love with a grown-up kind of love and who learned to love me in return. She is the one I married a few years later. She is Heather.

It all started at a party I threw in seminary. I invited some college friends to come down to it, and like all my parties in those days, the music leaned rather heavily on '80s new wave. My friend Liz noticed this and mentioned to me, "You know, Heather Painter likes eighties stuff as much as you do."

"Really?" I asked, interested. Liz was a junior at my alma mater, and Heather was a sophomore. Heather was involved in theater as well, so I knew who she was, but I wasn't sure we'd ever had a conversation. "Yeah, now that you mention it, she and I were the only ones wearing denim jackets, weren't we?" It was 1998, and denim jackets were not exactly the height of fashion at the time.

Liz nodded, "Uh-huh."

The next day, I emailed Heather. This started a two-week-long series of emails, essays really, about the joys of '80s music, '80s movies, and '80s fashion. But it became much more. These emails started to get deeper, and by Valentine's Day, I had asked her out, and we shared our first kiss in her dorm room.

We were about an hour's drive apart, and so I found ways and reasons to visit her just about every weekend for the next six months. I remember the night we walked up to Bowman's Tower in New Hope, and I told her I loved her. I remember the night a few weeks later in her dorm room when she told me she loved me too.

I also remember the weeks in between my confession of love and hers. I kept telling myself, repeatedly, *She feels the same way you do; she's just not as free with that word as you are.* I remember thinking that she'd better find that word soon or I wouldn't be able to hold it together. I was so grateful when those weeks ended. I remember telling her about my struggle with depression, and her response was: "That's okay. I love you, and I'll help you if I can."

I remember looking up in the stars one night that summer and seeing a very bright star right next to a crescent moon. I told

Heather, "That's us up there. The moon and star." I wasn't sure why, it just felt right somehow, and she agreed.

I remember just a week after that, driving with Heather and her parents to JFK airport, as we dropped her off there to catch a flight for a semester abroad in Ireland. I can recall the tearful hugs at the airport as we said goodbye for months.

I also remember my fall break from seminary that year when I traveled to Ireland to stay with her for a week. Heather had planned a trip for us to the Aran Islands, and she'd booked us a room in a hostel on Inishmore.

When we got off the ferry, we saw options for getting around the island: bus tours, bike rentals, and taxi cabs. We thought about our budget as students and decided to just walk to the hostel, which was about a mile away. No problem. We arrived there within half an hour. The hostel was more of a bed-and-breakfast, and Heather loved it. Our room was large and pink, and Heather was so beautiful as I watched her sitting in the large windowsill, looking out and enjoying the sites. She belonged in Ireland. The patient yearning of the Celtic islands fit her quiet thoughtfulness and her airy spirit.

The next morning, we decided we would see the whole island. It was only about nine miles long, so we figured we could walk. We spent the whole day walking. We held hands in silence for much of it, learning to communicate without speaking. We saw baby goats that made Heather giggle. We saw ancient Celtic Christian ruins that stirred up feelings of peace in me. We saw the tiniest snails that intrigued us both. And we saw the moon and star again. When we returned to the hostel, it was already getting dark, and we were exhausted. An incredible day, and it was such deep joy to share it with her.

I remember so many things from that first year together, but what I don't remember was the Mike Treatment. I never did that to Heather. Why not? I don't know. Was there something about her that prevented it? Or was I just older and more mature? Or did the Dark Voice just take a breather for a while?

If so, he missed a trick, but it did happen eventually, after we'd been together well over a year. We were sitting in her dorm room, and I told her, "I don't know why you're with me. I'm useless. You'd be better off without me."

She looked up from her cross-stitch and said, "Well, unfortunately for me, I'm stuck with you. Oh well."

The Dark Voice was speechless.

CHAPTER 19
THE SPECIAL GUEST

AGE 25

I got my Master of Divinity degree from seminary. That gave me the educational credentials to be ordained a pastor in the ELCA, but I didn't take part in the candidacy process to become a pastor. So what could I do with this degree? What on earth was I qualified for now?

Turns out I was qualified to work for the church in other capacities. I got hired as the full-time Christian Education Director at St. David's Evangelical Lutheran Church. When I started, I was so confused and bewildered about what I was supposed to do. I mean, I knew the job description, and I knew the tasks I was supposed to accomplish, but I had no idea how to do it. How would I reach out to teenagers and kids? How would I teach adults? What should I focus on?

One of the most challenging parts of the job was teaching confirmation class. This involved teaching twenty middle schoolers for about an hour and then sending them off into small groups led by other adults. We had a prewritten curriculum, and I usually tried to follow it as closely as possible.

The curriculum called for bringing in a special guest each week to talk for a few minutes about an experience in their own life that somehow connected to that week's topic. These guests were often very moving. I worked hard to find just the right person for each topic. There was a couple in the area whose infant daughter had died a few years earlier in a car accident with a distracted driver, and I invited them to talk about forgiveness. One week I invited someone active in Alcoholics Anonymous to talk about the evils of alcoholism. And then there was the week I decided to be the guest myself.

The topic that night would be one of the petitions of the Lord's Prayer: "Lead us not into temptation," also translated as "Save us from the time of trial." I was sitting in the old, shabby farmhouse I was renting at the time, thinking about what to do with this upcoming class. "Who should I ask?" I inquired out loud. The shag carpet and my beat-up and broken couch didn't answer me. My cat, Atticus, didn't answer me, nor did the three flies he was chasing. I looked around. *Man, this place is a wreck*, I thought. "Who should I ask?" I said again.

I realized that this place was perfect for me at that moment: thrift store furniture, dark brown 1970s paneling, windows without screens, and a roof that kept the rain out. It was analogous to who I was at age twenty-five—I was safe, I was sturdy, but inside I was so confused and messy. I still felt mixed up about who I was, what I was supposed to be doing, and what I believed, yet I *knew* the right Lutheran answers to do my job well enough.

I wasn't a danger to anyone or myself like I had been a few years earlier, but I wasn't exactly put together either. I was just as confused as I was as an adolescent. Is this what adult life was supposed to be like?

Then it occurred to me, and I shouted, "I should be the special guest next week!" Atticus jumped straight in the air and looked at me. I got up and thought to myself, *I should talk to the kids about my own temptations, my own trials. I should tell them that I'm no different than they are, and that it's okay to have these problems. It's okay to be screwed up. It's okay to be suicidal sometimes. I'll tell them, "In just a few years, you too could be an old, rundown farmhouse!"*

This would be the very first time I shared my story in a public setting, and I was nervous. How should I talk about it? What should I say? What if somebody got upset that I shared it? What if somebody there was going through something like what I went through—what if they had their own experience with the darkness? Well, then maybe I could be someone they would feel comfortable talking to, right? Right. This would be a good thing. It had to be.

Wednesday arrived, and I welcomed the kids to class. I was standing on the stage as I usually did and told them what the topic was: "Save Us from the Time of Trial." Then I announced, "Our special guest tonight is someone who has dealt with temptations and trials in his life but has gotten through them. Our special guest tonight is . . . me." I stepped down off the stage and sat down on a folding chair. (Sheesh. The melodrama.) I read them something I'd already written:

> When I was younger, I felt that I was evil, terrible, and that there was no way I could change. I saw myself tempted to be mean, to make fun of others, to insult and ridicule and disrespect them, and I thought there was no hope for me. I honestly thought the best way to deal with this would be to end my own life. That was a very powerful temptation for me, one I thought about for years, all throughout high school.
>
> Finally, one night my freshman year at college, I ended up in a tree with a noose, ready to do it. I knew what I was doing would hurt others, but somehow, I thought that it would hurt them more if I stayed alive. I had tears coming down my face, and I was ready to do it, ready to end it all, until suddenly I saw a light in the distance. I don't know what the light really was. I guess it was really a car or a house or a streetlight or something, but I saw it as a light of hope. A light that told me I didn't have to end it like this. That I shouldn't. I got out of the tree, and I never tried to kill myself again.
>
> I have since been depressed from time to time. I have since been down and felt worthless, but it never reached that point. I never came that close to ending my own life again, because, somehow, I know now that that's not an answer. No matter how bad the trials are in our lives, there are ways to get through them.

I know that sometimes the hardest trials in our lives aren't physical ones, but emotional ones. Physical troubles like diseases and car accidents are incredibly tough to go through. But I think for some of us it's even harder to deal with feelings of uselessness and meaninglessness in our lives. And God has an answer for that. It can be very difficult to hear God's word when we feel evil and terrible, but God's word is still there. I heard it through that light I saw and through friends and family later that week, as I started dealing with my suicide attempt.

I read them "A Believer's Prayer," the poem I had written while in St. James Hospital. Then I looked up at them.

A few were looking at me. A few were looking at their feet. A few looked out the window. I heard the crickets chirping out there. I got up, went back on stage, and continued to teach the lesson. I never brought it up with them again. Nobody ever approached me to say I might understand their pain.

But a few years later, I was speaking on the phone with the mother of one of the students. She said, "Daniel's been talking about suicide lately."

"I'm so sorry. Do you think he's serious?" I said.

The mother said, "I don't know, but I think it's because you talked about it in confirmation class. Why did you do that? You shouldn't talk about things like that."

My gut twisted up like a corkscrew. "I'm sorry. I had no idea that he would hear it that way."

"He sees you as a role model! You made it sound okay to kill yourself."

"Oh God, I'm sorry. That's not at all what I meant to say."

As it turned out, her son was (and is) okay. But I learned then that it wasn't okay to talk about this, at least not the way I did. I still hadn't learned that people take stories of suicide seriously. I also hadn't yet learned what it is to be a spiritual leader, that people look to you as a model for their behavior. I didn't take any time to process my story with them after telling it; in fact, I didn't even know that I *should* process it with them. The way I told the story was short and shoddy. "Hey, sometimes things are bad. Once they were so bad for me, I tried to kill myself. But I stopped myself. You can too. The end." There was so much more I could have said, should have said. There was a pregnant silence in the air, but I just stopped.

And after that phone call, I felt miserable.

You should have known better, an old voice whispered.

CHAPTER 20
NOT THE BEST MAN

AGE 26

I loved going to weddings in my twenties, especially those weddings that brought the old gang back together. For me, the core of the old gang was always Ryan, Amanda, and me. We had other friends, but our bonds were always closest with each other. And even after months or years apart, we could always just pick up a conversation where we last left off.

One beautiful day, my friend Jim got married at the Jersey shore, and the old gang was there. Heather and I attended, as did Ryan and his girlfriend, and Amanda and her fiancé. The ceremony was on the beach, a simple service with "Ave Maria" and a sand blessing. After the ceremony, we all walked down the road a block or two to the restaurant for the reception. The cocktail hour was a blast, and I had more than a little to drink. We all talked and laughed.

But some number of beers later, I found myself face-to-face with Amanda's fiancé, Gene. And for no obvious reason, I shoved my finger into his chest and said, "You know, she's very important to me. And you'd better treat her right, or I'll . . . well, I don't know what I'll do, but it won't be pretty."

I didn't scream it. It wasn't a record-scratch moment where the whole room turned to look. But Amanda noticed, and she was not happy about it. She grabbed my arm and said to Gene, "Excuse us. He and I need to have a little talk." She led me outside.

"Have you had a little to drink, Mike?" she asked me as we reached the sidewalk.

"Maybe a little, or maybe a lot-tle," I slurred, laughing at my hilarious joke.

She shook her head and said, "Let's walk."

She led me down the street back toward the beach. "That wasn't about Gene," she said.

The bright sun and the sea breeze were helping me get my marbles back. "No, of course not," I said. "I think Gene's great. I think he's really good for you." This was true. I didn't know him all that well, but what I knew was good. "Oh, crap. I'm really sorry for that. That was uncalled for."

Amanda slipped off her shoes as we reached the sand. We kept walking. She said, "It's not just that. You have been so punchy ever since he and I got engaged."

She was right and I nodded. I knew exactly what this was about, and so did she. It was about her decision regarding her wedding party. She and Gene had decided to break with tradition; instead of men on "his" side and women on "hers," they were planning a coed wedding party. Amanda was going to have a "man of honor" instead of a "maid of honor," and she was also going to have two bridesmaids and a "bridesman."

She had asked Ryan to be the man of honor and me to be the bridesman along with the two bridesmaids. The trouble was this—even in this unique arrangement, there was (to me, anyway) a clear hierarchy: the man of honor was top dog, and the bridesmaids and bridesman were lower. And it hurt because I always thought the three of us were equals in our friendship. It was now about six months since I'd found all this out, and there was still a year until she and Gene got married. This allowed lots of time for my emotions to fester.

She stopped and turned to me, gripping my shoulders. "Seriously, what's the matter with you, Mike? Why does my wedding party bother you so much?"

I bit my lip and kicked at the sand. "You know, I was joking in the beginning. Remember when we all met for dinner to celebrate your engagement? I kept making all these jokes about the wedding party. I really meant it as a joke. Or I guess I was trying to make it a joke because I knew I was being petty. But it hurt, you know? It hurt."

"What hurt?"

"It hurt because the three of us are supposed to be equals!" I sat down on a nearby bench and put my head in my hands. Maybe it was the beer, but I was crying a little. "I'm sorry."

Amanda sat down next to me and said, "Don't be sorry. Just get over it. I don't know what you think 'man of honor' means, but it doesn't mean I care about Ryan, love him, or respect him any more than I do you."

I looked straight at her. "I know. Look, I thought it was awesome when you decided that Ryan and I would both be in your wedding party. I love the idea that you have a 'man of honor' and a 'bridesman.' But when I found out that Ryan was one and I was the other, it felt like a slap to the face. That's why I didn't have Ryan as my best man in my wedding, so you two could be equal there. He was a groomsman, and you were one of Heather's bridesmaids. We even made sure that you two would walk together."

She smiled just a little. "And the gossip that started after that . . ."

I said, "Yeah, that was funny."

She took my hand. "Seriously, Mike. I am starting out on something brand new here. Marriage is scary to me. And I need all the support I can get. I need you to figure this out. I need you to cut out this crap. Will you do that?"

"I don't know why I've been so angry. Maybe it's time I get a therapist."

I looked out at the ocean. The tides were calm and steady. A few seagulls cawed and it sounded like they were laughing. "I'm sorry, Amanda. I'm going to get better. Thanks for not giving up on me."

"I'll be honest, Mike," she said. "Sometimes it's tempting." After a very uncomfortable pause, she turned to me and said, "But you're worth it." She stood up. "Let's go back to the party."

I stood up, and we hugged. I said, "I know that Ryan will do a much better job with the man of honor stuff, anyway. I'm no good at planning parties and stuff."

She nodded and quietly said, "Right. Do you understand now? It's not about him being a better friend or a better person, you idiot. It's about him being better at best man stuff."

We went back to the party.

A few days later, I wrote a letter of apology to both Amanda and Gene, explaining where my feelings were coming from, but also acknowledging that I was going to work hard to stop reacting the way I was. I also called a counseling center and began seeing a counselor regularly for the first time.

CHAPTER 21
HOT AND BOTHERED

AGE 27

It was hot, really hot. It was July, and I was in Georgia. I was sitting at a table outside a restaurant reading through the pages of a collection of lyrics from about twenty songs and making notes on them with a pen. I was looking for patterns recurring throughout the lyrics, making notes on which songs tied together with which others, trying to make some sort of narrative, and trying to find the perfect order for the songs.

It was my latest attempt at making a mixtape—the ultimate mixtape, in fact. This mix would define me. This collection of various songs by various artists would form the rock opera of Mike. It would be my finest mixtape, my finest collage, my finest creation. But this was just a distraction from the reason I was in Georgia.

I was in Atlanta with a group of ten youths and four adults from St. David's for the triennial National Youth Gathering of the Evangelical Lutheran Church in America. There were thirty thousand people who were excited to be in Atlanta for this event, but there was also me. I wasn't excited; I didn't want to be there at all.

I was in charge of our group. The other three adults looked to me to make decisions. It was understandable—I was the staff person, the Director of Christian Education. It was part of my job to oversee our group at events like this, but I really wanted to be home. I was used to being able to go home after my commitments at the end of the day. Here, I felt like I had to be "on" every waking moment for the five-day event, and maybe I was feeling a little out of my depth. I was only twenty-seven years old, and I was guiding these people from hotel to conference center and back several times a day, wrangling them and praying with them, teaching them and keeping them safe, disciplining them as necessary, and trying to laugh with them as well.

And it was too hot, too sunny, and too humid. As I sat there, I thought about what had happened the night before.

I was almost asleep in my hotel room with the two boys in our group, when a light knock came at the door. I crawled out of bed, walked to the door, and quietly opened it. It was Teresa, one of the other chaperones. Teresa's daughter was in our group, and Teresa was in some ways the mother of the whole group, the one who always had the compassionate yet firm word, the one who always watched out for everyone. "Hi. What's up?" I said.

"It's Bailey," Teresa said. Bailey was one of the youths in our group.

"What's wrong with Bailey?" I asked, trying to keep my eyelids open.

"Can you come and talk with us?"

"Sure." I gingerly closed the door behind me and walked down the hall of the hotel in my pajamas.

I followed Teresa to her room, where Mary and Dawn, the other two chaperones, were. When we sat down, Teresa said, "Mike, Bailey snuck out last night. And she's planning to do it again tonight."

"Snuck out? To do what?"

"To meet a boy."

I nodded. "How did you find out about this?"

Mary said, "Stacy and Jeannette told me. They're in the same room with Bailey, and they're worried about her."

They were all looking at me. What was I supposed to do? What were they expecting from me? After a few moments, I said, "Well, that's part of what these events are about, aren't they? I can remember sneaking out at one or two youth events myself."

Teresa leaned toward me and said, "Mike? Are you serious? This is serious!"

"Okay. I'm sorry. I guess I'm still waking up. What do you suggest we do?" I said.

"I was thinking that one of us should talk to her," Teresa said.

I interrupted, "Do you think that would stop her?"

She coolly added, "*And* I think one of us should sleep in her room."

"Okay," I said.

Mary asked, "Mike, would you talk to her? Teresa can sleep in there then. We'll have Stacy and Jeannette sleep in here with us."

"Let me think a moment." I put my head in my hands as though I were thinking, but that's not really what I was doing. I wasn't deep in thought, but deep in emotion.

A familiar voice paid me a visit. *You don't know what you're doing, do you?*

No, I don't.

You're supposed to be a leader here, and what kind of leader are you? The voice in my head persisted.

I never wanted to come here.

You never should have come. You're a fraud, and they'll see through you. They're seeing through you right now. Then silence.

I looked up and agreed to their plan. Mary went and knocked on the girls' room door. When Bailey came out, Mary brought her to me, and she and the other women went to get things ready for the room switch.

I asked Bailey, "How are you doing?"

"I'm fine. How are you?" she said.

"You know, it's really important that we get enough sleep at these events."

Bailey replied, "I know."

"I understand you were up a little late last night, out of your room. Remember that we signed a covenant to follow the rules?"

"Oh, I was just walking around because I couldn't sleep. Sometimes I just can't sleep. It's no big deal."

I was confident this was a lie, but I didn't have any evidence other than the other girls' words. "Okay. Can I count on you staying in your room tonight? If you can't sleep, maybe you can just read or something?"

"Okay," she said.

Through the whole conversation, Bailey was pleasant and agreeable, as always. Yet I knew that she was going to do whatever she wanted if she could get away with it.

Sitting outside the restaurant the next day, as I pored over those lyrics, I remembered all this—my useless conversation with Bailey and Teresa's scowl. I kept reading and jotting notes on the lyrics in front of me. I never wanted to come here. I had no idea what I was doing. And besides, I couldn't get my mind off what had happened the last time I was at a National Youth Gathering.

It was twelve years earlier, when I was fifteen. The National Youth Gathering that year was in Dallas, Texas, and it was just as hot and humid and not altogether fun for me. This trip there was also a group of four adults and ten youths, and among those youths were my great friend Ryan and my newly ex-girlfriend, Robin. The preparations for the trip took about nine months. As we prepared for the trip, doing fundraising and team building, I was so looking forward to it. To spend time in Dallas with one of my best friends and my girlfriend was going to be outstanding.

But then, just about a month before the trip, Robin and I broke up. And to make it worse, she and Ryan started dating almost immediately. I was stunned. Ryan didn't even talk to me about it. He just started dating her. I tried to stay friends with both of them. I knew that I was *supposed* to be okay with this.

What right did I have to stand between them? Isn't that what love means—to want the other person to be happy? My own feelings didn't matter. I'd just have to push those feelings down and get over them.

And so, just a few weeks later, still raw with these feelings of abandonment and betrayal yet still trying in vain to ignore them, I boarded the plane for Texas. My best friend and my ex were two rows behind me, and I was sure they were holding hands, laughing, and kissing. The whole plane ride was hard—I was supposed to be there with Robin.

The first evening in Texas, Ryan and I were in our hotel room, and he was on the phone with Robin, who was just a few rooms away. I slid the balcony door open, and stood out there looking down, out into the hot and noisy streets of Dallas. We were seven stories up. I wondered what would happen if I jumped.

The next day, our group went to a big festival area within the event called "Freedom Center." There were booths, games, activities, displays, and all kinds of things. Our group leaders told us we could split up, enjoy the festival, and meet back in three hours. Everybody went off in groups of two or three, but I went off by myself. I wandered among the games, watching as large and small groups of young adults from who-knows-where laughed and had a great time. I meandered among the food, not interested in any of it, then went over to a stairwell where I just sat and cried.

I sat there, in the center of what was for so many other young people a profound and life-changing religious experience, and I felt God's absence. I felt like I was in a desert—hot, dry, and waiting for the scorpions to come.

Twelve years later, I sat outside that restaurant in Atlanta, again in the center of what may have been a profound and life-changing experience for the youth in my care. I remembered my feelings from Dallas, and I remembered my failure the night before regarding Bailey.

I already knew the title of my ultimate mixtape: *Persona*. At the center of the epic musical would be the song "Persona" by Blue Man Group. Its haunting minor melody, slow hypnotic beat, and heavy percussion would form the heartbeat of my opera. The lyrics spoke of hiding from something buried deep in the past, hiding every day behind masks upon masks upon masks. That song seemed to represent exactly who I was in Atlanta that hot, hot week. I was hidden deep within myself, hidden from the hot sun because the sun was too frightening. Everything around me was too frightening. I kept scribbling in the margins of the lyric sheet. At least I knew what I was doing with those lyrics. I felt in control there.

CHAPTER 22
LOCKED IN

AGE 28

It was about 9:00 p.m., and I'd been at St. David's for about three hours at that point. Only eleven to go. It was free time now, and the twenty or so teenagers at the church were running around, eating snacks, talking, and laughing. A few latecomers arrived and I sighed. I was hoping that those two wouldn't show up. But there they were, walking into the Fellowship Hall a few steps ahead of their father. Dave and Joe, two brothers I just wasn't in the mood for that night. They were in eighth and tenth grade, if I recall correctly. They each carried a sleeping bag and a small duffel bag.

I said, "Hi guys, you can bring your stuff in here." I led them into one of the Sunday School classrooms where all the other boys' stuff already was, sleeping bags aimed in every possible direction. As Dave and Joe unrolled their sleeping bags, I looked over my shoulder to see that nobody else was in the room. Then I said to them, "Listen, you two. I don't want any crap from you tonight."

Dave said, "I don't know what you're talking about."

Joe said, "Okay."

They walked out into the Fellowship Hall and started to play games with the others.

The night went on. I led a few games and a Bible study. I had to tell Dave and Joe to pay attention a few times. A few extra chaperones arrived around 11:00 so we could all carpool to a bowling alley for midnight bowling. I scolded Dave and Joe when they tried to hang out in the arcade instead of bowling with the rest of us. We returned to the church for more games and then a quiet worship service at 2:30 a.m. And then came 3:00. The time I'd been dreading. Bedtime. Every year at this sleepover event (called a lock-in), some of the youth would refuse to sleep. And every year I would make a judgment call between letting my anger out and just letting them be themselves.

I wished everyone a good night, and the girls went into their room with their chaperone, while I was with the ten boys. I turned out the lights and lay down on the blow-up mattress I'd brought. (I found it so hard to sleep in the church, and I was hoping the blow-up mattress would help.) I heard some talking and laughing. No problem, it was only 3:05. I'd give them time. The talking got louder. Okay, 3:10, time to tell them to sleep. "Good night, boys," I said loudly. It quieted down for a minute. Talking. Laughing. A bang as something hit the wall—a shoe, maybe? "Hey!" I shouted. "What was that?" I could feel the anger welling up, the *indignation*. How dare they!

Now general rustling started to drift into farting noises. I looked at my watch. 3:30. That was enough. Something had to be done. I wasn't sure who was being loud, who was quiet, or who was the ringleader. And I knew I'd never be able to find out. I just had to make an example of somebody. I got out of my sleeping bag and stood up. "Joe and Dave, get up. Get your stuff. You're sleeping out in the hall with me."

"But I didn't do anything!"

"This isn't fair!"

I set my mattress up just in front of the door, so I'd notice if anyone tried to go in or out. I pointed to arbitrary spots on the hard floor of the Fellowship Hall. "You sleep there, and you sleep there."

They looked at me with disdain and fury. They stomped off to where I told them to go. They stayed quiet. I fell asleep around 4:00 or so.

I awoke at 6:30 when a few parents arrived to make breakfast for us. The kids were all still sleeping. I wandered over to the kitchen. "Sleep well?" one of the parents asked.

I just shook my head.

"Ah," she said. "Coffee will be ready in five minutes."

I gave her a thumbs-up and ambled to the bathroom to change and brush my teeth.

When I came back, the youth were starting to stir. I invited them to come have breakfast. There was coffee, juice, cereal, and bagels for everyone. I hunched over a bowl of Cheerios and thought about what I would do when Dave and Joe's parents came to pick them up. I had two options: tell their parents what happened, or just let it go. I decided to let it go. I thought I was doing them a favor. This way they wouldn't get in trouble with their parents. I figured they'd appreciate my choice, and honestly, I didn't feel like dealing with it anymore. End of story.

Not "end of story."

A few months later, I was at a congregation council meeting where Dave and Joe's mother, Jill, was on the council. Before the meeting started she asked me if we could meet afterward for a few minutes. I said that would be fine.

After the meeting ended, Jill and I walked down to my office and sat down. "So, what's up?" I said.

"My boys are very upset with you about what happened at the lock-in. They don't want to come to church at all anymore," she said.

My heart seized in my chest. I knew this feeling. I hated this feeling. "I'm so sorry," I said. "Can you tell me more about this?" My words were so carefully chosen, but inside I could feel the magma starting to churn. The Dark Voice was listening very carefully.

Jill said, "It's not just the lock-in. They're good kids. They're not as bad as people say they are. I think you just don't know how to relate to them. Maybe there's a course or something you could take to learn more about how to relate to teenagers."

That stung. I'd been working with teenagers at this church for four years. The piercing pain in my heart grew, enveloping me. I could still see Jill; I could still see my office, but I was suddenly looking from a distance, like the scene was happening at the end of a long dark tunnel. I heard a voice speak within the darkness.

Did you hear that? She just said you're incompetent. She just said you don't know what you're doing. She's right. You should have known better. But there's no course that would help. This didn't happen because you're uneducated. You have plenty of book learning, more than enough to know how to handle this. No, this happened because you're a broken, horrible person. You should have known better.

I licked my dry lips, ready to speak. The voice inside my head shouted at me:

Hold on! Don't you dare show that this is hurting you. Then she might actually feel sorry for you. It's her *family who is suffering unjustly here, not you. You deserve to be punished, and they deserve to be vindicated.* Internally, I nodded in understanding.

On the outside, I said, "Again, I'm sorry. I would like to find a way to make this right. Do you think it would help if I reached out to them?"

Jill looked surprised. "Maybe it would. I didn't expect you to say that."

I continued, "What if I sent letters to them, telling them I'm sorry, and offering to try to rebuild a relationship with them?"

She nodded. "I don't know. That might be good. Thank you for offering to do that."

She left my office, and I walked over to the door and turned off the light. As the light in the room was extinguished, I felt as though all the walls were closing in on me. I sat down on the hard floor, the cold tiles matching the cold I felt inside. I heard the voice echoing around me on every side:

You have prevented these two boys from attending church.

You have single-handedly prevented them from hearing the good news of Jesus.

But they were troublemakers! I had to discipline them! I tried to argue back.

No! You had one job here. Tell them about Jesus. And you failed.

You were far worse than ineffective. You had an effect. A terrible one. You are worthless. You are worse than worthless. You are evil. You have done something unforgivable.

And you. Should. Have. Known. Better.

I know, I sobbed. I'm so sorry.

A few days later, I wrote the letters and mailed them. I followed up with a phone call about a week after that. I never heard from either of the boys.

PART FOUR
KEEP AWAKE

CHAPTER 23
THE BELLY OF THE WHALE

AGE 29

I think of Jonah as my patron saint. Jonah was called to be a prophet to proclaim God's will to people. One particular day, he was called to proclaim that will to the people of Nineveh, a wicked city east of Israel. Jonah, however, did not want to do that. So he ran away, boarding a boat heading for Tarshish, a port at the far end of nowhere, due west of Israel, exactly the wrong way. Yet God did not take no for an answer; God pursued Jonah and eventually caught him in the belly of a whale, wherein Jonah experienced a great peace and knew the presence of God. After that, God called him again to go to Nineveh, and this time Jonah followed directions.

My journey toward being ordained a pastor in the Evangelical Lutheran Church in America has some similarities with Jonah's journey. This became clear to me in the belly of my whale, which was a retreat in New Jersey for pastors and other church workers.

Five years into my career as a Christian Education Director, I was getting burned out in the position. Certainly conflicts, such as what happened at that lock-in, were part of it. But that wasn't all. I loved the congregation, but I no longer loved the work. My job was complex: I was expected to spend eighty percent of my time doing Christian Education stuff (Sunday School, youth group, Confirmation class, and so forth), and twenty percent doing pastoral assistant work, including pastoral care and visitation, as well as occasional preaching and worship leadership.

I was finding that I found more pleasure and meaning in the pastoral elements of my work, and less and less in the Christian Education stuff. I found meaning in preaching and leading worship and in visiting the sick and homebound, sharing some hope with them. But I dreaded organizing ski trips for the youth group. I still loved getting to know the teenagers—praying with them and sharing hope with them. I just didn't want to be in charge of the programming. I knew that every job had parts you liked and disliked. But eighty was a lot bigger than twenty.

And that scared me. I felt very stuck. I couldn't imagine leaving St. David's for another church—I would just be doing the same work in a different locale. And I didn't think it was possible to find a position that was in line with my joys, since I wasn't ordained. I wasn't a pastor, and I would never be a pastor—that was absurd. Who wanted that level of responsibility? Who wanted to be a lightning rod for everyone's frustrations? Who wanted to be where the buck stopped? I could never, ever do that. Never. So, what options did I have? None.

But then the retreat happened. Right at the height of my burnout, I attended a four-day retreat for new Lutheran church professionals and pastors, held at a Roman Catholic retreat center in New Jersey. The retreat was designed as an experience to help young and inexperienced church leaders grow in their confidence and their roles. While I was there, I had a powerful experience during which God threw me on the ground and told me to shape up. But it was God, so it was done with grace and love.

Shortly after checking in at the Retreat Center, I felt the urge to walk around outside, and I found a small cemetery on the center grounds. There were a few inches of snow on the grass, but the paved path that led around and through the cemetery had been cleared. It was a five-minute walk to make a loop around it, and it felt special. The snow was covering the lower portion of the tombstones, so I could not read any of the names, but dozens of white crosses poked through the snow. I didn't know who these people were, but something about this little cemetery was holy. I felt I was in the presence of greatness here. I walked about five or six loops and then went back in the building. I found myself coming back to that cemetery over and over again throughout the retreat.

I walked and walked and walked around, and as I walked, I began to hear a still, small voice speaking to me. I wondered if I was hearing the voice of God. The voice told me things like this:

"It's time to stop screwing around."
"It's time to listen to me."
"It's time to accept this."
"It's time to let me break through this enormous wall you've built."

I began to see that over many years, I had built a wall around myself. A wall that said in big letters, *NO PASTORS ALLOWED*.

Each afternoon and each evening of the four-day retreat, I walked around that cemetery. Over the course of the retreat, the snow melted, and along with it, so did my wall. As the snow melted, I was able to read the names on the tombstones more clearly. They were nuns. They were all nuns. Of course they were—this retreat center had originally been a convent. So this cemetery was a tribute to hundreds of nuns. I was walking in the footsteps of generations of women who answered God's call and who heard God's voice and responded. My own conversation with God continued as I walked. Over the days, I experienced exchanges like this:

"I saw you made peace with a former classmate today. I'm glad you did that."

Yes, she forgave me.

"I forgive you too. When can you forgive yourself?"

And this:

"I heard six people telling you today you should really be a pastor."

Yes, they're all crazy. People have been saying that silly thing for years.

"Interesting."

And this:

"I saw you in that conflict management workshop this afternoon when you asked, 'What if I'm the one causing all the conflict?' Did you hear the leader's answer?"

Yes, he said that then there's hope. He said that if you recognize that you're doing that, it means you're ready to change.

"And did you hear when he talked with you later and laid his hands on your head, offering you forgiveness?"

I think so.

And finally this:

"The retreat is over. Go home now. I will have more to say to you there."

Like scales falling from my eyes, I finally saw what had been happening for years—I had actively stopped myself from becoming a pastor. I had actively thrown roadblocks in my own way. I had actively built this wall. I'd vigorously prevented myself from even considering such a path. And why? Out of fear. Fear that I wasn't good enough. Fear that I would not be able to handle the responsibility. Fear that the life of a pastor was something for people other than me: people more stable, people more confident, people less broken, people who were just . . . better.

But God reached out to me in New Jersey and said, "Enough. It's time to tear down this wall."

Finally, the retreat ended. I packed up my belongings and called my friend Matt. His apartment was on my way home, and I wanted to talk to somebody about this. "Matt," I said. "It's Mike. I'm in New Jersey, and I'm going to be driving near your place in about forty-five minutes. Can I stop over and visit with you for a bit?"

"Sure! I'd love to see you," he said.

I drove to his apartment, thoughts and feelings swirling in my head. When I arrived, he welcomed me in. He lived alone on the second floor of a building right on the main street of town. He gave me a big hug. "Can I get you anything? Cup of coffee? Beer?"

"Coffee would be great," I said.

He went into the kitchen and started brewing a pot. I looked around the living room. There were books everywhere. He was an avid reader and was now a journalist for a small-town newspaper. I pulled a book off the shelf. Matt walked into the room. "Don't read that one, Mike. It'll only depress you."

I looked at the cover and laughed. "Really? I think I need more depression in my life, actually."

He took the book from my hand and put it back on the shelf. "No you don't, buddy. You've got that angle all sewn up." The coffee maker gurgled loudly. "I'll be right back." He went into the kitchen and returned with two full mugs. "Still take it black, right?"

"Is there another way to drink coffee?" I asked. I sat down on the couch, and Matt sat across from me in a big beige papasan chair.

"So what brings you out here, anyway?" he asked.

"I was on a retreat with a bunch of clergy-types." I sipped at my coffee and then put it down. "Matt?"

"Yeah?"

"Matt, are you a pastor?"

He got a confused look on his face. "Umm, no . . ."

I said, "Right. Is that because you've always said 'no' to being a pastor?"

He laughed a little. "No, Mike, that's not why."

I nodded. "I think I'm starting to figure some things out."

Matt just looked at me with a quizzical look on his face.

I said, "I think I'm supposed to be a pastor."

Matt looked up and then nodded. "It makes sense. You'd be a good one."

I said, "Really? That makes sense to you?"

He shrugged. "Yeah. I mean, you've always loved the church, and you're a good leader. I mean, why not?"

I shook my head in disbelief. "Am I the last one to know this?"

Eventually I went home and talked with Heather about all of this. She was surprised but excited for me. She said, "If this is what you want, then I will support you all the way. What's the first step?"

I said, "Well, I'll have to call the bishop and talk with him. Hopefully I can start a candidacy process pretty soon to get the ball rolling. I never did CPE or an internship during seminary, so I guess I'll have to do both of them. I don't know what else this will entail."

"What's CPE?" she asked.

"I'm sorry. I spend so much time around clergy! It's Clinical

Pastoral Education. It's like being a student chaplain at a hospital. It's usually three months in the summer. Between that and internship, we will probably have to move."

She took my hand. "If this is what you're supposed to be doing, then I'll follow you anywhere." After a moment, she added, "You know, I'm so in awe of you sometimes. I don't know what it's like to feel 'called' to something like you do."

I said, "Is that what this is?"

A few days later, I called the bishop. It was remarkable how smoothly things worked out. It was like I'd been going down the *up* escalator for years and now was finally done fighting against the current. Allowing myself to go with the flow gave me a sense of spiritual vertigo. Everything happened so quickly. Almost overnight, I was in the candidacy process. I was registered for a unit of CPE at a behavioral health center just a mile from my home, which would start in just four months. I was also set up for a year-long internship that would immediately follow.

I was finally heading toward Nineveh, and it felt good. The Dark Voice had kept me heading to Tarshish for years, telling me I was not good enough to be a pastor, that I was not good enough to be what God wanted me to be. But in the belly of the whale, the only voice I heard was God's, and it changed everything. At least for a while.

CHAPTER 24
NEGATIVE NOLAN

AGE 29

Clinical Pastoral Education (CPE) is a mandatory program for all students in the candidacy process toward ordination in the ELCA. It can be done full-time in a few months, or part-time over a longer period. During the program, a student will spend some time as student chaplain at a clinical location, often a hospital or some other healing center, and some time in a classroom setting with a supervisor and a small group of other students. The classroom portion of CPE is designed to be intense, as a supervisor and peers dig deep into the ministry each student is doing in their clinical time, trying to discern what's good, what needs to be improved, and what shows from a student's own psychological baggage. Many of my seminary classmates reported hating CPE.

Nonetheless, I went into it with a hopeful attitude. The CPE program I entered was a ten-week, full-time program at a behavioral health center called Penn Foundation. I was glad to be doing this at a place that worked with mental illness and addiction. I hoped that along the way, in addition to growing in the skills necessary to be a good pastor, I would also be able to wrestle with some of my own demons.

I had a complicated placement at Penn Foundation. It included some time with folks in a group home and some time in a house for people who had dual diagnosis (both a mood disorder such as depression or bipolar as well as an addiction to alcohol or drugs). I also spent a few hours a week in the ER and ICU of the hospital across the street.

But perhaps the most powerful part of my placement was as the chaplain at Camp Courage, a day camp for kids with various behavioral health diagnoses or who were on the autism spectrum. This day camp was held in the woods at a Mennonite camp just a few miles away. I was there to share some stories, lead a Bible lesson with the kids, and also to be with them throughout the day, responding as necessary to any spiritual needs the campers or counselors had.

I'd had a pastoral role at camps before, but they were always church camps, so my role was a given. At a church camp, connecting everything you do with faith in God is normal and expected, so a chaplain there functions kind of like the "theological expert in residence" to help the staff make those connections. But Camp Courage was run not by a church, but by a mental health center, so the spiritual component wasn't baked into the program in the same way. My function at Camp Courage was more to offer individualized spiritual help to kids who needed it or asked for it. One challenge for me was to notice these needs, another was to make sure that any spiritual support I offered was in line with a camper's own spirituality and not just to assume a Lutheran viewpoint.

I arrived on the first day with some trepidation. I wasn't sure if the staff of the camp were particularly interested in my role. I wasn't sure if the counselors would view spirituality or religion as important, or even welcome. I was unsure if the counselors would view me as a peer, an authority figure, or an interloper.

As it turns out, they were happy to see me. They saw me as a unique yet important part of the staff, and if nothing else, they were glad to have an extra pair of hands if one of the kids needed some extra care. I clicked immediately with one kid. He was nine years old, short, stocky, and he wore thick glasses. He carried an inhaler and used it regularly. And he was a loner. All the kids were there because they had behavioral health issues; many of them had trouble relating to other people. But in my eyes, this one was a loner even among loners.

On the first day, I did an icebreaker game to learn the kids' names and a little bit about them. We all sat in a circle, and we each had to come up with a word that described us that started with the same letter as our first name. I started with myself: "Mellow Mike." As we went around the circle, I met "Kind Kimberly," "Energetic Erin," and more. Then we got to the loner. He was sitting sideways in the circle, looking away from the rest of us. I said, "Hey, it's your turn. Could you turn and face the rest of us?"

He turned his head toward me, looked down, and said, "I'm not playing."

I said, "Come on, it's just your name and one thing about you."

He said, "It's Nolan."

I said, "Okay, great. Hello, Nolan! Now can you think of—"

He interrupted me. "Not-even-existing Nolan."

I tilted my head. *Oh boy, what do I say to that?* "That's pretty clever, Nolan. But how about something else?" I looked around the circle and asked, "Can anybody think of a different name for Nolan?"

One of the girls said, "How about 'Nice Nolan'?"

Nolan shook his head and said, "Whatever. Fine." He took a puff from his inhaler. We continued the game.

Apart from the inhaler, I felt like I was looking into a mirror. Nolan reminded me so much of my childhood self. Luckily for me, my CPE class had just attended a workshop on transference (when a client unconsciously directs feelings he or she has for a significant person, like a parent, onto the counselor) and countertransference (when a counselor unconsciously directs similar feelings onto the client). This helped me recognize what was going on within me. Instead of getting caught up in a swirl of nostalgia and emotion, I was able to use that swirl to help me relate to and minister to Nolan.

I took a special interest in him and made sure to find opportunities to talk with him. One particular walk I took with him on a Tuesday inspired me to write a poem.

> Negative Nolan
> Doesn't want to be at camp
> It's raining outside us both
> And inside Nolan

Michael J. Scholtes

Negative Nolan
He introduced himself that way
He said, "not-even-existing" Nolan
We suggested "nice Nolan"
And he grudgingly accepted
He let us move on to the next person

Nolan and I talked about camp
"I want to go home"
We talked about friends
"I never wanted to come"
We talked about the rain
"I knew something bad would happen"

I saw here before me
Negative Mike
My nine-year-old self
A boy I remember quite well
A boy still imprisoned inside me

So we talked about God
I told him it's raining on me too
We talked about Job
I told him, "God loves you"
But he had an answer for everything
Just like Negative Mike
It might work for others
But never for me

I want to go home
I wonder if the counselors will let me call my mom

Negative Mike
Knew the answer for help
The answer was no
Just like his name
Negative Nolan
Recited the same way
While the pastor-in-training floundered in the rain

I finally said, "Nolan, I have to go
But I've really enjoyed our talk
I hope that I'll see you on Wednesday
Promise me you'll consider coming Wednesday."
He said, "Well, maybe just that one day."

The pastor-in-training drove off wet and tired
Remembering how no words would work with
Negative Mike
But remembering a face or two
Who cared enough to share them
Maybe, just maybe, I can be a beacon of light
I cannot save him
I cannot convince him
But maybe on Wednesday I can wait awhile
With Negative Nolan

This was a rare moment when I really felt like I could see what I looked like from the outside and see just how challenging it was to try to reach me. I wasn't able to exorcise my own demons through Negative Nolan, nor did I try. But I was able to gain some compassion for him and for myself.

And he did come back on Wednesday.

CHAPTER 25
ANNUNCIATION

AGE 29

When I was finished with CPE, I still had one more major learning experience before I could be ordained: a one-year internship. I served this at a church called Hope Evangelical Lutheran Church, which sat on top of a hill with a stunning view of the Blue Mountain. I was the full-time student pastor (or vicar), and I had the opportunity to pretty much do everything the pastor did. Of course, I had already done a lot of this before at St. David's, but now I had a dedicated supervisor (Todd, the senior pastor of Hope Church) with whom I met every week to process, to plan, and to laugh.

I remember one of our first meetings, not long after I started. I was sitting in Todd's office. My chair had its back to the large window, which meant that whenever Todd looked at me (or anyone else he was meeting with) he could see that beautiful mountain view. A good trick, actually; that probably helped keep him smiling, no matter the conversation.

"So, there's something I probably should tell you," I said.

"Oh boy, here we go," he said, playing with a pen. "What did you say to the women's group yesterday?" He laughed.

"Nothing, honest! Why, what did you hear?"

His smile went away. "Why, what did you say?"

"Nothing," I said. "That's not what this is about."

He muttered something and pretended to throw his pen at me.

"Seriously, though," I said. He put the pen down and made eye contact with me. I continued, "Maybe I should have told you this before I got here, but either way, you should know now. I have a history of mental illness. I've lived with depression for most of my life."

He nodded. "I'm not surprised. Lots of pastors do."

I said, "I just thought it was important for you to know."

Todd said, "I don't need to know about that. That's nobody's business but yours unless you choose to share it. Except . . ." He paused, tapping the desk with his fingers. "Except, that since you brought it up, and I thank you for trusting me to do that, I just need to know that you're working on it with someone."

"Oh, absolutely," I said. "That's one of the reasons I'm bringing it up today. I want to make sure I can still go to my counseling sessions every three weeks."

He blinked. "Of course you can. That's your health. That's the most important thing you can do. So long as you're taking care of it, there's no reason we need to talk about it going forward unless you want to."

Todd was very supportive of me, and a few months later I decided to make use of that support.

It was December, three months into my internship, and I hadn't yet shared anything about my illness with the congregation. I was scheduled to preach on the Fourth Sunday of Advent (the last Sunday before Christmas). The gospel reading was Luke 1:26–56, the Annunciation, when the angel Gabriel announced to Mary that she would soon bear a child who would save her people. As I studied commentaries to prepare a sermon, I found a deep connection with Mary's faith and fear.

I brought this up in Todd's office during our supervisory session the week before. "So, I was looking at the gospel for next Sunday."

Todd said, "Yes, the Annunciation. I don't know why I'm letting you preach that day. I love Mary!"

I shook my head. "You're such a Roman Catholic, Todd."

He gasped in mock offense.

I continued, "Actually, I was noticing something here that I wanted to run by you. Mary is so frightened, yet so full of faith at the same time. I was thinking of a connection between this and the time I attempted suicide when I was seventeen. But I wanted to see what you thought about sharing that publicly in a sermon."

"Hmm," he said. "I can see the connection. But you want to be careful how you bring it up."

"I know," I said. "I talked about it once at St. David's with a confirmation class, and I don't think I did it the right way."

We talked about what I did wrong then and what I could do better this time. He told me it was important to frame it as something in the past. "Congregations like to see their pastors as human, as vulnerable. But they don't like to worry that their pastors are fragile, or that they're not up to the job." And he told me to be prepared to deal with some conversations about it afterward.

I ultimately decided to tell my story. This is an abridged version of the sermon I preached that day.

I'm going to tell you two stories about faith in the face of fear. The first is the story of Mary. We don't always think of Mary as fearful, but let's look closer. Mary was a young woman, probably in her early teens, who was engaged to a man named Joseph. She was looking forward to being married in less than a year. In fact, her whole future depended on the marriage occurring, and if anything went wrong before the wedding, such as becoming pregnant, then she could be cast out and have no future.

So when the angel Gabriel appeared to Mary bringing good news that Mary would conceive a child who would save the world, do you think this was good news for her? What would this do to her? To Joseph? To her family? Gabriel told her, "Do not be afraid" (Luke 1:30 NRSV). But Mary was most certainly afraid. Full of fear.

And yet Mary said to the angel, "Here am I, the servant of the Lord; let it be with me according to your word" (Luke 1:38 NRSV). Sounds full of faith. Mary's trying, really she is. But what did she do right after the angel left? She hit the road. As fast as she could, she went to see her relative Elizabeth. Maybe she was looking for advice. Maybe she was trying to put some distance between herself and Joseph, to think about how to tell him. Maybe she was just running scared, looking for companionship.

We don't know what she was looking for, but here's what she got. Elizabeth welcomed her, told her that she was blessed. Elizabeth was overjoyed that Mary would come to see her. She confirmed what the angels had told Mary. And then Mary proclaimed a deep faith. "My soul magnifies the Lord, and my spirit rejoices in God my Savior" (Luke 1:46 NRSV). *Her* Savior. God's angel had told Mary that she would have very, very difficult times coming. God's angel told her that she would never have a normal life. Yet she proclaimed this God to be her Savior.

Through a divine message, and through her relationship with Elizabeth, she was able to proclaim that God's news was indeed good. Was she still scared? Terrified. Think about it . . . wouldn't you be? But she was given something far stronger than fear: deep, deep faith.

Here's my second story about faith in the face of fear. It's about me. This was twelve years ago. I was seventeen.

When I was younger, in high school, I struggled with depression and with self-confidence. I was scared . . . scared of myself. I was scared that I was hurting people. I was scared that I hurt my friends, that I hurt my family, that I was unable to do anything right. I was scared that I always said the wrong thing, always forgot to be sensitive to other people's feelings, always failed when I was needed. I wanted to stop hurting people. And I tried. I tried to change. I prayed for strength, for compassion.

It didn't work. No matter how hard I tried, I couldn't accept that I was good enough. So I decided that the second-best thing I could do, if I couldn't change, would be to go away forever. So, one cold night in November when I was a seventeen-year-old freshman at college, I walked down to a local park and climbed a tree with the intention of hanging myself. I prayed for strength. I didn't want to do it. I didn't want to die. I was scared of dying. I was scared of pain. But I was more scared of the hurt I could cause other people if I kept living. So I walked, and I prayed. I climbed that tree, warm tears streaming down my face in the chilly night. I got the noose around my neck, and I reached up to wrap it around the branch above me . . . I saw in the distance a light.

I saw a light. A light shone in the distance. It was bright. It was bright white, and low, right along the western horizon. It came out of nowhere. There had just been darkness, and now, a bright light. I don't know what it was from a physical sense. It might have been someone turning on a porch light. It might have been a distant streetlamp. It might have been a bright star that just peeked out from behind a cloud. I don't know. I don't care. Because I know what that light was for me. That light was an angel from God. A messenger who told me, crystal clear, "No. Do not do this. Climb back down."

And I did. I climbed back down, and I walked back to my dorm room. I crawled into bed. The next few days were a blur. I didn't tell anyone about it for days because I was scared. When I did finally talk about it, I ended up in a psychiatric hospital for eleven days.

My life was forever changed in those eleven days. The doctors and nurses were great. The other patients I lived with for that time were great. But, you know, the most powerful thing for me, the thing that made the most difference, were my friends and family. I got visits from so many. Phone calls from others. Cards from others. They were devastated that this had happened but overjoyed that I hadn't succeeded.

I saw that I was wrong about myself. I saw that I was worthy of love and that I truly was receiving love. I was overwhelmed, overwhelmed with joy. I saw that, yes, I hurt people. But they didn't leave me. They forgave me, and they wanted me to get better, and they loved me. What that light in the western sky told me, I now knew for sure. I was loved, and I was going to be okay.

I didn't tell you this story to get your sympathy. I didn't tell you this story to bare my soul. And I didn't tell you this story to scare you. This happened twelve years ago, and I've gone through counseling, and I'm not climbing trees anymore.

I told you this story to show that faith is possible in the face of desperate fear. I told you this story not so you could see me climb the tree, but so you could see me climb back down.

Do I still say stupid things sometimes? Yes. Do I still hurt people sometimes? Yes. That's part of being human. Do those things scare me? Sometimes. But I was given such a gift twelve years ago. I was scared, but God came to me through a light and through my friends and family. I was given faith that I was loved and that God will use me. And this is good, good news. That light is what kept me alive for a few more days. That faith is what keeps me alive today.

Mary was scared, but God came to her through an angel and through Elizabeth. She was given faith that she was loved, and that God would use her, and that this was good, good news.

That light of the world that Mary bore—the one we'll celebrate in this place in just a few days—is real. I saw it. It saved my life. I don't say it's real because I saw it, but because of the faith God gave me through my friends and family. I know that God loves me and has plans for me. And that's true for you too.

Are you scared right now? If you're scared of something, it's okay. But let me assure you, the light of the world is coming, and it is coming to give you faith. Faith in the face of your fear. Faith that's stronger than any fear you have. Amen.

The nave (worship space) of Hope Church is built in the round, and I preached this sermon from the floor, rather than staying in the pulpit. Todd had taught me how to slowly walk around the space as I preached in order to connect with the most people. As I walked, I noticed that all eyes were more attentive than usual. One woman, Margaret, was nodding along with me and crying. In that room, I was surrounded by people listening and reacting and responding not only to my words, but to my emotions. I was in the midst of people who cared.

When I sat down next to Todd after the sermon, he put his hand on my shoulder and said, "Good job. Good job."

Afterward, many people told me that the story was very meaningful to them. Several people told me I was brave. One man told me, "I know where you've been. I've been there. Thank you for saying that today."

That day I realized that maybe this pastor thing could work out. And maybe my history could even help.

CHAPTER 26
O'ER BETHLEHEM

AGE 30

It was November 30. I could not sleep, so I walked around Bethlehem.

I was in a one-year holding pattern. I had completed CPE. I had completed my internship. But I couldn't be ordained yet because I was doing this all out of order, and there were some processes that hadn't yet lined up. Committees had to take votes. There were i's still to be dotted, t's still to be crossed. I had to wait, and I was told it would probably be about a year from when I finished my internship until I would be settled in my first call as a pastor.

Heather and I had to find a place to live for that year, and I had to find a job. Finding a place to live was challenging because we were looking for a place that was willing to go month to month with rent and would allow our three cats. Finally, we found a house for rent in a less-than-ideal section of the city of Bethlehem. But hey, it was a roof.

I was able to get an almost full-time gig at St. Robert's Lutheran Church as the director of family ministry. It was more or less the same work I'd done at St. David's for five years, the work that had burned me out. St. Robert's was an inner-city congregation, and during my time there, I learned that I am not best suited for inner-city ministry. Youth ministry in the inner city, at least in my one-year encounter with it, struck me as very different than youth ministry in the suburbs. One of the most challenging things was keeping the kids' attention. I prepared programs that went completely off the rails when absolutely none of the kids would pay attention to me.

I was also used to being able to contact parents to let them know about behavioral problems, but for a number of the kids I encountered at St. Robert's, the parents didn't really take on parental roles. Some neighborhood kids hung out at the church, not because they were looking for faith, but because they were looking for a safe place or even a meal. The ministry we did with them was so vitally important, but it wasn't a perfect fit for me. Often, I felt unprepared, unskilled, and useless.

Looking back, it was a good experience for me to have. But at the time, it didn't always feel that way. There were moments when I loved the congregation and the job, and there were days when I was overwhelmed with anxiety.

November 30 was one of those days. Or rather, one of those nights. I laid in bed, my mind racing. Heather was breathing slowly next to me. There was a cat on the bed with us, snoring quietly. It wasn't Heather or the cat keeping me awake. It was fear. Fear about the job. Fear about the future. Fear about whether I'd ever be ordained. Fear about when it would happen. Fear about where in the country I'd end up going when I was assigned in a few months. Fears and fears and fears. Insomnia was a companion I'd known for some time. I was long used to being awake far past my bedtime about two nights a week. The Dark Voice liked to whisper at night.

On this night, I had had enough. I wasn't going to lie there awake. And I wasn't going to just sit around the house either. Not that night. I decided to go for a walk. I threw on a T-shirt and jeans, and I walked out the door. Yes, a T-shirt and jeans. On November 30. Because it was seventy degrees out. In Pennsylvania. On November 30. At 11:15 pm. If you're not from Pennsylvania, let me assure you—that is ridiculous. It should have been about forty degrees. Snow wasn't unheard of for the end of November. Seventy degrees? Absolutely ridiculous.

I crossed the bridge over the Lehigh River and walked up and down the streets of North Side. I was sweating. Sweating on November 30. And not from exertion, but from the heat. Did I mention it was November 30?

I knew this part of town fairly well. The streets were wide, and the neighborhood always gave off a sense of sophistication and education. I walked past a dormitory my sister had lived in while she was in college. I walked past an elite prep school. I walked past the beautiful, sprawling campus of Central Moravian Church.

I walked within blocks of the apartment where a few of my old college friends lived. They were probably up at this hour. But I wasn't interested in seeing them. I was here to talk with somebody else because I was angry. Angry at God for getting me into this mess. I didn't want to live here. I didn't want this inner-city job. And I didn't want to be waiting for this long, waiting with so much uncertainty about the future. I wanted some answers. I wanted some clarity. *I want it to be cold, God! It's November, God!* I looked at my watch. It was 12:10. *Ten minutes after midnight, which means it's December now! Why is it so hot? In December?!* I didn't really yell in the middle of the night as I walked up and down the streets. But inside, I was screaming at God.

Why did you do this to me? What are you trying to accomplish? Why do I feel so alone here? Why can't I sleep? And why is it so hot?

I felt paranoid and abandoned. My anxiety was so ramped up, I couldn't think straight. I was walking so fast I was almost running. I suddenly realized I was in the middle of an intersection. I hadn't even noticed I was crossing Broad Street. If it hadn't been the middle of the night, I could have been killed. This only made me angrier. I finished crossing the street and picked up the pace.

Fine! I shouted internally to God. *Fine! You want to do this to me, fine! But please, please, I beg you, please at least show me a sign that you're here. Show me you're with me through this!* I knew I was overreacting. I knew that I was having some real "first-world problems," as Heather would say. But the anxiety was tearing me apart. And I needed to know that God was with me. And then—

It started to rain. It rained. December 1, at 12:30 a.m., it started to rain in Bethlehem. It was wonderful! I was walking down New Street in the rain in a T-shirt, and it felt amazing! It felt cleansing. It felt like renewal. It felt like baptism. It felt like life! I started laughing and crying because I saw this rain as a sign that God really was there. God wouldn't take the unseasonable heat away, but God would send rain into it. God wouldn't take my anxiety away, but God would send hope into it. I felt that hope. The hope felt like rain. I walked home laughing and crying at the same time, tears mingling with rain. When I got home, I went to sleep. And it was a good sleep. Anxiety would return many times over the next few months, but for that moment, it was quiet. For that moment, hope dissipated the anxiety.

It was December 1, and I slept.

CHAPTER 27
MY SHADOW, MY SOUL MATE

AGE 32

My anxiety, as usual, was wrong. Everything worked out, and I was ordained. I was even assigned to the Northeastern Pennsylvania Synod, which was my hope. I became the pastor of a congregation called Our Savior Evangelical Lutheran Church in a small town not far from where I grew up. It was so exciting to finally be realizing my "spirit dream," as a friend called it, to at long last be fulfilling the calling that I'd ignored and rejected for so long. The people at Our Savior were great. The job was mostly what I expected. Life was good. Jonah's journey was complete. I was the pastor God wanted me to be—I guess.

But completing this journey didn't fill the hole in my heart. I was still struggling. I was still scared of the unknown. I was still anxious. I was still depressed.

My therapist had helped me recognize where in my body my anxiety manifested itself, and I discovered that there were two sensations that tended to happen. One of them felt like a hand on my head, squeezing. The other was a tight, clenching sensation in my chest, as though my heart was being squeezed. Both of these sensations distracted me from the outside world, distracted me from the issue at hand.

I was ordained, but the squeeze was still there, strong as ever. I started writing poetry again for the first time in years. Here are two of the poems I wrote that first year at Our Savior.

DOUBLE

My shadow, my soul mate
You've always been my double
Squeeze my head, clench my chest
And lead me into trouble

You're beside me
From the very first day
You tie up my knots
Interrupting my play
Never lonely
For you are right here
I want to awaken
Without any fear

I evade you
I want to be free
I claw you
The more you claw me

You never moved out
Please take a day off
I tried smoking you out
Now I've developed a cough

I'm a leader
But you are my boss
Melt down my trophies
They're nothing but dross
God may be triune
But I am just two
A cold frightened child
And you, always you

My shadow, my soul mate
You've always been my double
Squeeze my head, clench my chest
And lead me into trouble

NEVER ENOUGH LEFT
I'm scrabbling upward to heaven
I'm clawing alone through this rock
I've never been one to feel lonely
But I just can't deliver this flock

I'm torn apart waiting for guidance
I'm tossed aside sifting out sand

I've never been one to feel hardened
But life is a long ampersand

I'm garnishing wages from science
I'm tarnishing ashes and tin
I've often been one to feel guilty
But there is no recycling for sin

There are too many roads that I walk down
Too many people to see
Too much riding on these lines
Never enough left of me

CHAPTER 28
CUTTING THE CORD

AGE 33

Heather and I had been married for seven years when we decided it was time to try to have our first child. I'd been hesitant—as much as I liked the idea of being a father, it was terrifying. I always wondered if I was mature enough, if we had enough money, and if we had enough time. Plus, I knew that mental illness is hereditary, and I wasn't sure I wanted to pass this on to another generation. We thought about adopting, but the more I looked into that, the scarier the wait, the uncertainty, and the expense became to me.

When Heather became pregnant, everybody—parishioners, friends, family, colleagues—had something to say about it. And through all their unsolicited yet well-intentioned advice, one thing became brutally clear to me:

Everything.

Was.

About.

To.

Change.

I heard that over and over again.

"Having a child changes everything."

"You won't look at anything the same way again."

"Everything changes in little ways."

"Nothing will ever be the same."

And on and on.

I started to think that when my daughter was born, the sky would be burnt orange. The leaves on the trees would be bright silver, and pterodactyls would soar among them. The laws of physics would be suspended: perhaps the earth's magnetic field would invert, the ocean levels would rise, clocks would run backward, and black licorice wouldn't make me gag.

For someone fearful of the unknown, this anticipation was monstrous. I grew increasingly anxious as the day got closer. I became obsessive about all kinds of things. For example, my congregation had offered me two weeks of parental leave to begin when my daughter was born. Of course, we didn't know what day that would be. So, in order to be ready, I drew up documents and spreadsheets that outlined in great detail what would have to happen if she was born on this day, or that day, or the next. It was like the nerdiest "go bag" ever. The closer and closer her arrival came, the more the maw of the unknown gaped at me. I was scared.

The day of my daughter's birth was not great. I had a video camera, and I filmed some conversations between Heather and me throughout the day. After ten hours of hard labor by Heather, my daughter wasn't progressing the way she should, and the videos were filled with more and more frustration. I was by Heather's side through it all, and as her pain and frustration amped up, I got more and more upset, more and more anxious.

The anesthesiologist was working so very, very slowly to get an epidural started, and when he inserted the line into Heather's back, she cried out. I squeezed her hand and said, "It's going to be okay. This time the epidural will work." I looked up at the anesthesiologist. "It will, won't it?" I snapped at him, my voice laced with barely contained rage. This was the second time they'd tried to give her an epidural; the first one provided no help at all.

The anesthesiologist looked at me with cold eyes and said, "They're not one hundred percent, you know."

This continued another two hours. Heather cried and clung to my hand. I tried to be compassionate, and I tried rather less successfully to keep my cool when talking to the midwife and the nurses.

Finally, they stopped trying. The midwife and the anesthesiologist and the nurses in the room all stepped back from the bed. The midwife said, "We're going to have to go to a C-section. It's just not going to happen this way."

I looked at her with disbelief. "Then why did you put her through this for so long? What was the point?"

Heather said, "Mike, please calm down."

Within minutes, she was being wheeled away to be prepped for surgery. A nurse told me, "We'll be back for you in about twenty minutes. You can be with her for the actual procedure. Here." She tossed a gown, a mask, and gloves on a table. "Put those on, and we'll be back soon."

Those twenty minutes were agony. I sat on a chair in the birthing room. I grabbed the video camera, pointed it at myself, and started talking.

"I'm tired right now. I'm really tired. I'm really scared. I'm scared that I just don't have enough in me to take care of her and of the baby the next few days. I'm scared that I don't have enough in me to take care of all the things I need to. And I'm also scared that this isn't the end of this day. I'm scared that there are gonna be complications in surgery. I'm scared . . . I'm just scared."

In that ellipsis, I thought some things that I couldn't say out loud, not even to my own video camera. I was scared that Heather would die. Or the baby would die. Or something else would go horribly wrong. I was scared of going home a single father. Or going home with Heather but without a child. Or going home alone. I couldn't handle any of these thoughts. Everything was indeed about to change. But not the right way. This was not right. This was not right. This was not right. This was not right.

Finally, a nurse came. I followed her to the operating room, sat next to Heather, and held her hand. A curtain was draped from a bar above us to Heather's chest. It was just me and an anesthesiologist on our side of the curtain. It seemed like forty doctors were on the other side. Heather was nervous and cold, and I held her hand tightly for a while as the doctors did their work.

After a few minutes, I heard the cry of an infant, and someone said, "Come here, Dad! Meet your daughter!" Heather was still cringing in some pain and shivering.

I shouted, "I'm staying here with my wife!" I was so upset that I couldn't even be bothered to meet the newest member of my family, Zoe. I don't know if they offered me the chance to cut her umbilical cord. I didn't care.

But within an hour, the three of us were all back in the birthing room, safe and healthy. Everything was going to be all right.

Within a few days, the three of us were home. Everything was going to be all right.

But it wasn't. Heather bonded with Zoe immediately, but I didn't. I was unable to console her when she cried. When she was calm or sleeping, I found it a pleasure to hold her, but the instant she started to fuss or cry, I was lost. Nothing I did worked. Her cries went right through me; I had no patience or compassion for her. I would get angry and fed up quickly. Heather was rapidly recovering from her surgery, so I felt more and more useless and worthless.

I started to resent Zoe. The definitive moment happened one night when I went to change her diaper. I was having trouble with it, and she was squirming and wailing. After getting the diaper on, I held her against me, hoping that rocking her and whispering to her would calm her down. It didn't—in fact, she got worse. I was overwhelmed with anger and emotion. I pulled her away from me quickly, too quickly, and put her down. As I pulled her away, I heard her scream. I looked down, and the stump of her umbilical cord was caught on my sweater. I had pulled it off. Now, looking back, it was probably just about ready to fall off anyway, but that's not what I felt at the time.

I felt like I had just abused my child. It was like the night I had grabbed Anna too tightly, but worse. So much worse. I ran out of the room and told Heather she had to take care of Zoe. I went into the living room and started to cry.

Two days later, my sister Christy flew in from Seattle to stay with us for a few days. One night, she asked me how I was doing.

"Not well," I said. "Did you know that men can get postpartum depression?"

"Really?" she said. "I never heard about that." We were downstairs in the den. Zoe was asleep in her bassinet on the floor, and Heather was napping upstairs.

"Yeah," I said. "I looked it up, and it's not nearly as common in men as in women, but it happens. I found a forum online for awareness and support for men who have it."

Christy nodded. "So you think you have it?"

"I don't know. But I'm definitely much worse than I've been in a really, really long time. Heather doesn't need me, and it doesn't seem like I can do anything for Zoe. And now with you here, I feel like there's nothing at all for me to do. I've been crying a lot. I feel absolutely worthless and useless. I've actually been thinking about going on meds."

"You're not on any meds? Really?"

I shook my head. "Other than Saint John's wort a few years ago, I haven't ever taken anything. I've always been scared of the side effects."

She said, "They're not as bad as they used to be."

Zoe started to fuss a bit, and Christy got up from the couch and walked over to the bassinet.

I was surprised to hear her say that. I asked her, "Are you taking meds?"

She nodded without looking up. She was giving Zoe her pacifier, and Zoe was calming down again. "I don't really have depression like you do, but I've had some pretty nasty anxiety in the past few years. It's really helping, but it took a while to find the right cocktail." She got up and returned to the couch. "In fact, sometimes family members respond well to the same drugs."

She told me the particular medications and doses she took, and I wrote them down.

Over the next week, I discovered that psychiatrists were very hard to find. I made phone call after phone call, and they all had wait times of around three months for an appointment. I remember speaking to one receptionist and explaining that I thought I had postpartum depression. She corrected me saying that it was something only women got. She said, "Maybe you mean post-traumatic stress disorder?" Sigh. I finally gave up trying to get a psychiatrist and went to my family doctor. He agreed with my sister that her cocktail was a good place to start and wrote me a prescription. And after a few weeks, it helped. At least I think it did.

It's so hard to tell with mental illness. Depression and anxiety are such slippery and fungible things. There are no lab tests to determine what effect the meds are having—it's all about your own reports. It's all in your head, when it comes down to it.

I did not, after all, have male postpartum depression. It was my regular garden variety depression, triggered in a big way by Zoe's birth. The Dark Voice used that trigger to tear me to shreds inside.

Not everything changed after all. The sky was still blue, and the Dark Voice was still loud. Same old me.

But now I had a newborn daughter, and after a while I did bond with her. I'll never forget the first time I heard her laugh. It was the day before Easter and Heather was napping, so I was alone with Zoe in the den. She was about three months old, and I had now been on antidepressants for a little over two months. They didn't cure everything, but they did give me something of a baseline. I still heard the Dark Voice, but it was easier to put him to the side.

I was holding Zoe while I practiced the Easter gospel reading for the next day. With her tiny body in my arms, I said, "The women had been saying to one another, 'Who will roll away the stone from the entrance to the tomb?' When they looked up, they saw that the stone, which was very large, had already been rolled back."

Suddenly Zoe laughed! I looked at her and said, "Is that funny? Yes, it's funny, isn't it?"

I continued, "As they entered the tomb, they saw a young man, dressed in a white robe, sitting on the right side."

She laughed again! I said, "Yes, it's a very funny story," as I laughed with her. I was finally falling in love with her. It was going to be okay. Being a father was going to be okay. And the new meds didn't hurt.

CHAPTER 29
ASKING FOR A CUP OF COLD WATER

AGE 35

For my first four years at Our Savior, I never mentioned my mental illness publicly. I was trying so hard to just be a pastor, and I was hesitant to open up and show any vulnerabilities. At first, this seemed like a reasonable professional boundary, and perhaps it was. But over the years, it started to feel less like a boundary and more like I was hiding my true self. I felt like I was always wearing a mask, never able to talk freely about what was going on inside me. I felt false, fake, like an impostor.

I thought about what would happen if I told the congregation I had a physical illness. I knew they would show compassion to me and not judge me for it. But mental illness carries a stigma—it's not the same as diabetes or cancer. Many people don't treat you the same if they find out you have a mental illness. They don't know what to do with it. They don't know how to talk about it. Tell people that you have cancer, and they all rally behind you and bring casseroles; tell people you have depression or bipolar, and they avoid you, not sure what to say.

This congregation was my home. In a way, they'd become a family for me. And I was tired of hiding an important piece of myself from this family. I was so tired of wearing the mask. I decided it was time to reach out and try to talk about it.

So one Sunday in June, I took off the mask during a sermon. It felt like the right day to do it. For one thing, we were meeting in our "summer chapel," aka our downstairs Fellowship Hall. The main worship space at Our Savior was not air-conditioned. It got brutal in there in the summer, so we were in the habit of holding worship downstairs for the summer months. It wasn't an ideal room for worship: it was a bit cramped, and the ceiling was low. We sat on folding chairs instead of wooden pews. The pulpit and altar were makeshift—a podium and a small wooden table—yet there was something very intimate and cozy about meeting in this space. Taking off the mask in that space instead of upstairs felt like opening up at a family gathering rather than a formal worship service.

It was also a day when we were holding our monthly healing service, a special part of worship in which people came forward if they desired. I would lay my hands on their heads and pray for healing, and then anoint their heads with baptismal oil, saying, "Receive this oil as a sign of healing and forgiveness in Jesus Christ."

The gospel reading that day was this:

> Whoever welcomes you welcomes me, and whoever welcomes me welcomes the one who sent me. Whoever welcomes a prophet in the name of a prophet will receive a prophet's reward; and whoever welcomes a

righteous person in the name of a righteous person will receive the reward of the righteous; and whoever gives even a cup of cold water to one of these little ones in the name of a disciple—truly I tell you, none of these will lose their reward (Matthew 10:40–42).

This is an abridged version of the sermon I preached:

Today's gospel talks about welcoming. Recently, we have been striving to make this congregation a place where people are welcome—where people who are hurting and vulnerable, people who are looking for something, can be welcomed so they might find comfort and hope and healing among us. That's a wonderful, wonderful thing.

But Jesus is talking about even more. This is the end of a speech in which Jesus is sending his disciples out into the world to share the good news. Here he tells them that as they go, some people will welcome them. And when they do, he himself will be there in that moment. In fact, God will be there. When someone welcomes a disciple, that person welcomes God.

But *we're* Jesus's disciples, so he's actually talking about *other people* welcoming us. And if other people are going to welcome *us*, then *we* need to recognize our need to be welcomed. *We* need to recognize that we need help. That we need support. That we need someone to give us a cup of cold water sometimes.

I'll start. I need your help. I need you to welcome me. Here's why. I have struggled with mental illness for most of my life. I live with a mental illness called depression. Mental illness is not as obvious as physical illness, but it is just as real, and it can be devastating. My depression is not severe, but its effects on me are real. Sometimes it takes away my ability to enjoy life. Sometimes it takes away my ability to take risks. Sometimes it takes away my ability to laugh, my ability to roll with the punches, my ability to relate to other people. Sometimes I make poor choices and overreact because of this illness.

I need help, and I do receive help. I see a therapist regularly. I take prescription medication. But today I ask for your help as well.

My depression often manifests itself through my own voice, my own voice telling me terrible things about myself. This voice is very cruel. The voice tells me that I'm supposed to understand everything. The voice tells me that I'm supposed to always be in control of myself and in control of my situation. The voice tells me that I'm very smart, and because of that, I should be able to solve any problem. And when I can't, the voice tells me I'm a failure. In fact, the sentence this voice loves to say more than any other is this:

I should have known better.

I share this with you not for sympathy. Not as an excuse for my mistakes. But I share this with you because you can help. I need your help. You can help by simply calling me on it. If you see me getting stuck and overreacting, you can ask me, "Are you having a 'should have known better' moment?" And believe it or not, hearing that actually helps me sometimes. Not always, but sometimes hearing that enables me to quiet that voice down, at least for a while.

It's very hard to ask for help. It's a risk. Because I've now told all of you one of my weak points. You can use this information to help me or to hurt me. I have to trust you, and I do.

Just a few minutes ago, I offered you healing. Now I'm asking you for healing. We can't fix each other, but what we can do is welcome one another as disciples. Welcome one another when we are weak and when we are thirsty. And that's enough. Because Christ promised to be there in that moment. And that is where real healing comes from.

And so I ask you to welcome one another and take the risk of allowing others to welcome you. Christ will be there.

The reaction to the sermon was not what I'd hoped. Nobody talked about it. I remembered back to when I shared my suicide story when I was on internship at Hope Church. So many people there spoke to me about it afterward, but not here. Nobody ever took me up on my invitation to call me out on a "should have known better" moment. On the other hand, nobody told me I shouldn't have talked about it. I didn't notice anyone treating me differently. It seemed like they just didn't want to talk about it.

Perhaps they just didn't want to think about it.

Maybe what Todd had told me was right, that people didn't like thinking of their pastors as *currently* having a problem. At Hope, I framed it as something from the past; here, I was honest that it was still very present. Maybe I'd made a big mistake talking about it.

See? You never should have mentioned it.
That was a mistake, opening that door.
You should have known better.

CHAPTER 30
MOMENT OF FIRE

AGE 35

The phone rang. I answered it. "Pastor?" said the voice on the other end.

"Yes," I said.

The voice identified herself. She was an active member of my congregation. "Did you know that the Brunners' house is on fire?" The Brunners were also members of the church, and they lived just across town. I was shocked—their house had just received devastating flood damage a few weeks ago.

"No, I didn't," I said. "Oh my goodness. They just got flooded!"

"I just thought you should know."

"Thank you very much," I said and hung up.

I felt paralyzed. My heart beat fast. My head felt clenched. I knew exactly what I would do any other week. I would just walk down there, see what was going on, spend some time with the family, and try to figure out how the church could help them going forward. But it wasn't any other week. I was on vacation for two weeks. Even though I hadn't left town yet, I was off duty. That was important to me. And it changed the equation completely.

The moment stretched into an eternity. Time slowed down to a stop. The outside world froze, and . . .

I hear two voices in my head. They are each telling me what to do. I know exactly who these voices are. They're the voices of two of my role models, two pastors I respect who have taught me a lot. I have been blessed with great pastoral role models over the years, from my father to my college chaplain, from the senior pastor at St. David's to my supervisors on internship and CPE. In these early days of ordained ministry, I often think of these role models. There are so many new experiences, so many new questions that I've never dealt with before. I often try to discern what to do by asking myself, "What would Dave do?" or "What would Maritza do?" or "What would Dad do?"

But there is no single model for how to be a pastor. And sometimes these voices in my head disagree with one another. Today, two of them disagree loudly. Pastor One says very clearly, "Go to the house right now. Yes, you're on vacation, but you're still home. Of course you should go." In real life, I know that Pastor One has done several funerals while on vacation over the years, because in his mind that's just what you do.

Pastor Two says, equally clearly, "Don't you dare go to the house. You have another pastor covering for you. Call her right now and tell her. Then don't give it a second thought." I know that in real life Pastor Two would do just that. In fact, he probably wouldn't have answered the phone in the first place.

When I worked with him, I asked him once, right before he went away on vacation, "Under what circumstances should I call you?"

He said, "None."

I said, "What if the church is burning down?"

He said, "Then they'll need a well-rested pastor to help them through it afterward. I trust the people covering for me."

I see the faces of both Pastors One and Two in my head, staring at me, waiting for me to decide, and I know that one of them will judge me harshly. I don't want to disappoint either of them. What do I do?

Then another face appears in my mind—the face of my current therapist, Stan. I started to see him shortly after arriving at Our Savior, mostly because I was feeling unworthy and confused about how on earth I could do this job. Ever since the retreat, I was looking forward to being the pastor, the leader. Now I just want somebody to tell me what to do. I want a handbook or a Sherpa. Instead I get Stan, who introduces me to existential therapy. He tries to equip me with tools and resources to make my own meaning, find quality in my life, and embrace my freedom to make choices. I find that I don't want all those things—I want easy and simple answers—but perhaps what Stan provides is what I need.

Over the years I meet with him, Stan gives me all kinds of homework to do. At his suggestion, I try to deliberately make mistakes during the day, to explore how that feels. I take a road trip to a small town about thirty miles away, just to sit by the river and think. I read Sartre and Camus, Kierkegaard and Tillich. I watch The Seventh Seal.

Stan never seems curious about the voices in my head, whether they're internalized versions of other pastors or the more familiar and *constant Dark Voice. Instead, he's curious about what I do when I hear them. He isn't interested in helping me be happier; he's interested in helping me to find meaning and quality. When I consider antidepressants following Zoe's birth, I ask his opinion. He doesn't give me anything except, "Well, that's your choice." When I consider moving to a new congregation, he's more interested in talking about the dilemma itself than about helping me to make the right decision.*

In my mind, Stan's face eclipses Pastor One and Pastor Two. He reminds me that there is only the present—no past or future. This is all we have, and I have to make a choice in this moment. And then he is gone, and it is only me. The decision needs to be made now. There is only this one moment. There is only me.

I make the decision. I will go to the house and spend some time with them. I will pray with them and make sure they have a place to go. Then I will tell them that I will be away for two weeks and that I will ask the covering pastor to check in on them. I will call that pastor and then try to put this behind me for two weeks.

I know I will second-guess myself. I know I will feel judged by the phantom pastors in my head. I know the Dark Voice will have some choice words. But there is only now. And this is the best decision I can think of now.

Time began to move again, and I got my shoes on and left the house. I could see the smoke in the west. I started walking.

CHAPTER 31
NAMING YOUR SUFFERING

AGE 37

It was Transfiguration Sunday, the day each year when we hear anew the story of Jesus leading Peter, James, and John up a mountain (Luke 9:28–36). On top of that mountain, Jesus was transfigured before them, glowing and dazzling. Moses and Elijah appeared before them, and then a voice from a cloud said, "This is my Son, the beloved. Listen to him!'" And then Jesus led them back down, and they began the journey to Jerusalem, the journey to the cross.

I have always loved Transfiguration Sunday. In the calendar of my tradition, it's the great hinge of the church year. It always falls in February or March, on the last Sunday of the Epiphany season, the season of light. Three days later, Ash Wednesday arrives, the beginning of the season of Lent, the season of walking to the cross. Transfiguration Sunday is the day that moves the church from one season to the next, from light to journey.

The brightest light ever, the most glorious reveal ever—Jesus on that mountain—moves quickly to Jesus walking back down the mountain, on the way to Jerusalem, the way to the cross.

It was my first Transfiguration Sunday at Living Grace Lutheran Church, my second call as a pastor. I was still enjoying the honeymoon period that pastors often have for the first year or so in a new parish, the blissful first months in which everything seems wonderful. Pastors and congregations are on their best behavior, enjoying the newness, the potential, and the excitement that this period brings. And so perhaps that was on my mind as I prepared for Transfiguration Sunday. Perhaps I saw myself on the mountain with Jesus, enjoying the view with Peter, James, and John. And perhaps I saw that this was an opportunity to talk about the sober reality of who I was.

It's funny. I waited four years at my first call to talk about depression, but I "came out" to my second call in less than six months. Maybe I just decided that I wanted to know where we stood. So, I preached a sermon in which I was honest. It went kind of like this:

> Linda's life was a mess. She just couldn't get a handle on it. Everything felt complicated. She was treading water, but just barely. She never really came to worship anymore, but I would run into her in town from time to time. Each time I saw her, Linda said, "Oh, Pastor. I'll get back to church when I get my life together." And I believe she meant it. She wanted to be back at church, but she felt that church was for people who had it together. And that wasn't her. Not right then. This is

the sermon I wish I could have preached to Linda. That I wish she could have heard.

In today's gospel, Jesus is glowing. Like lightning. On a mountain, glittering, glowing, glorious. And the disciples were overwhelmed. They didn't know what to say. And then a voice from a cloud said, "This is my Son, my chosen one. Listen to him!" Listen to him. Jesus was talking with Moses and Elijah, and they were talking about his death. His suffering. This glittering, glowing, glorious Savior was talking about suffering.

Reminds me of when God appeared in a glittering, glowing, glorious burning bush and spoke these words to Moses: "I know the sufferings of my people. I have come down to deliver them."

On the mountain of Transfiguration, Christ looks to the cross and says to you, "I know your sufferings. And I have come down to deliver you." And then Christ comes down from the mountain and begins the journey to Jerusalem, where he will be betrayed and killed. The glory of Transfiguration only lasts a moment. It's a glimpse of the real glory that comes through the cross. Through his suffering. Through his death. Listen to him. That's where he's going.

That's where he meets us. I wish Linda could hear that. I wish she could know that Christ isn't up on the mountain, waiting for us to clean up our act and climb up there with him. He's on the cross. That's where he meets us. In our suffering. In our brokenness. He came not to heal those who are well, but those who are sick.

And that includes us all.

I wish Linda knew that everyone in her church knew suffering. Everyone in her church knew confusion, pain, and worry. Just like everyone here does. Maybe then she would know that the church isn't a place you go when you finally get it together. It's precisely the place you go when it feels like you never will.

I wonder if her church family could have talked about that more. I wonder if *we* could. I wonder if we could talk more about our suffering, our brokenness? I wonder if we should? I think maybe.

So I will start. I'll tell you right now one of the ways that I know suffering.

I have struggled with mental illness for most of my life. I live with a mental illness called depression. Mental illness is not as obvious as physical illness, but it is just as real, and it can be devastating. My depression is not severe, but its effects on me are real. Sometimes it takes away my ability to enjoy life. Sometimes it takes away my ability to take risks. Sometimes it makes it hard to laugh, to roll with the punches, to relate well to other people. Sometimes I make poor choices and overreact because of this illness. I need help, and I am receiving help. Through talk therapy and prescription medication, I am living with my illness.

I don't tell you this to get your sympathy. I don't tell you this so that you'll worry about me. I certainly don't tell you this to make you uncomfortable. I tell you this because I think maybe God's people need to talk to each other and listen to each other about the suffering we know. I don't know what it is to have your suffering. But I know what it is to have mine. It's okay for me to stand here and tell you that. It's okay for us to talk about our suffering in church. Because our suffering is precisely where Christ comes. I need Christ to come to me when my depression flares up, to pick me up and hold me, until I am eventually able to get back on my feet. I need Christ to meet me there.

And he promises he will. And so far, he has.

You are suffering. You know you are. You know where you are weak. You know where you are broken. You know where you need to see God.

I invite you to name that out loud.

This is scary. This is a risk. I know. I invite you to name your suffering out loud now if you want to. You certainly don't have to. Mine is depression.

Here I gave them the opportunity to call things out. There was a pause, and then I heard someone say, "Depression." Someone else said, "Cancer." Someone else said, "Worry about my kids." Someone said, "Diabetes." I heard dozens of people, dozens of diseases, worries, fears, and the word "depression" at least five times. I continued:

Thank you for your courage. Whether you said it aloud or not, you just named your suffering. That's good, because truly I tell you, that is where Christ is going. We just saw him on top of the mountain, glowing and glittering and glorious. But listen to him. He isn't staying there. He is going straight to the cross. Straight to your suffering. And there he will bless you. And there he will heal you. And there he will bring you new life. And that is why we are gathered together here. Why we sing and pray and receive his body and blood. Because he's coming to us where we need him. This is God's Son, the Chosen. Listen to him. Amen.

I was *floored* by what happened in that pause, that moment when I invited people to share. This was the response I was hoping for. Better than I was hoping for. And it lasted.

People started talking about it. Not in a gossipy way—at least not as far as I know. But people started talking to me about depression. Some told me that it was very brave. Some told me that they understood what I was going through. One told me that he really didn't understand at all what depression was but wanted to talk to me to learn more. In my years at Living Grace, I continued to talk about it. And over the years, I believe that my honesty helped to lessen the stigma around mental illness within this congregation. I kept a list of local counselors on hand at my desk, and I lost track of how many people I shared that list with. People routinely checked in on me to see how I was doing. When someone at Living Grace asked me, "How are you doing?" I knew that, at least in some cases, they really did want an honest answer to that question.

After Robin Williams died, there was something in the air that made people across the country interested in talking about mental illness. I worked with two women at my church—one with depression, the other bipolar disorder—to plan an evening called "Light in the Darkness." The three of us each shared our story, and then we took questions from the audience. About fifty or sixty people came out to hear and learn. This was a congregation where I was welcome, despite my illness. A congregation where I was welcome *to have the illness* and talk about it. This was where I belonged.

CHAPTER 32
UNRECONCILED

AGE 40

I have always held a very strong opinion on the question of whether LGBTQ people should be accepted in the church. The answer is yes, yes, a hundred times yes. Accepted in every way. Marriage, ordination, everything. I have never understood what the issue is. They're people just like me. What business of mine is it whom they love or how they love?

One of my roommates in college came out while I lived with him, and I saw him berated and demeaned by one of the Christian fellowships on campus. It broke my heart. Three of my pastoral role models have been gay, and I saw two of them treated very shabbily by portions of their congregations because of it. It broke my heart. A very active college-age member of Living Grace came out shortly after I arrived, and two years later, she was hired by the congregation as our minister of music. I was delighted that the congregation didn't seem in any way bothered by having a gay organist. She was still the same person as the little girl they'd seen grow up just a few years earlier. This did *not* break my heart, and I was so glad to be serving at such a place! They welcomed me, and they welcomed her!

That acceptance was now being put to the test. It was a long time coming actually. Way back when I was new at Living Grace, even before I came out as depressed, two very active members of the church, Susan and Debra, had approached me.

"Pastor," Susan said, "we'd like to talk with you about something."

Uh-oh. I always got paranoid at openings like that—I always assumed they were upset about something I'd done. I tried not to let that fear show. "Sure. What's up?"

Susan continued, "We were wondering how you would feel about Living Grace becoming a Reconciling in Christ congregation."

Wow, it was a breath of fresh air to hear that. Reconciling in Christ (or RIC) is a designation that ELCA congregations and other church organizations can claim in order to publicly proclaim that they welcome people of any sexual orientation or gender identity. Many mainline Protestant churches have similar programs. Every congregation says "we're a very welcoming place," but LGBTQ people have learned that this is quite often less than true. Self-identifying as RIC and publicizing a welcoming statement is a way to announce clearly that *everyone* is welcome, even people who have been made to feel unwelcome elsewhere.

I smiled and said, "I would love to be the pastor of an RIC congregation. I'm not sure I'd love being the pastor of a congregation going through the process, though."

Debra said, "What do you mean?"

I said, "I'll be honest with you. I'm not a fan of dealing with church conflict. And this is likely to cause some."

Susan said, "Oh, I don't know. We're a pretty progressive congregation."

I smiled again. "Maybe you're right. Either way, I've only been here a few months. I really don't want to deal with this during my first year here. I need to build up some more trust. But let's talk about it again in a while."

They must have marked it on their calendars, because the day of my first anniversary as their pastor, Susan came into my office and said, "Pastor, let's talk about Reconciling in Christ."

I laughed and said, "Wow. You didn't wait. Have a seat. I've been thinking about this actually. And I think it's important that I'm not in a leadership role in the process. I think it will work best if it comes from you and isn't seen as a mandate from the pastor. You know I support becoming RIC, and I will share that support publicly at the right time, but I think to start I need to be rather quiet about it." I knew that something like this had to be seen as grassroots and not some edict from above.

Despite what Susan had said last year, I knew there would be at least some conflict, and I had to be at least somewhat neutral so I could help manage that conflict. Besides, I was called to be the pastor for everyone here, no matter their views on this. I decided that I would start as a cheerleader for the *process* of talking about it. And I hoped I'd know when the time was right for me to share my feelings on the matter.

She said, "That sounds fine. Debra and I were talking about it, and we think we have a good committee ready to go."

Susan and Debra, along with about four others, formed the Reconciling in Christ core group, and they started their work very slowly, too slowly. Every six months or so, they would remind the congregation that they existed. Perhaps they would have a ten-minute talk in worship. Or perhaps they would remind people they could answer any questions the congregation had. It just wasn't going anywhere, though.

Finally, after close to two years of little action, I encouraged them to step it up. I helped them create packets of information. I led several Bible studies on what the Bible really says (and doesn't say) about homosexuality. I organized a pulpit exchange between me and the pastor of a congregation that was already RIC. We got some people from our synod's LGBTQ taskforce to come out and answer questions during the Sunday School hour. And we provided two opportunities for open discussion with the congregation. These discussions were designed to be independent of one another, basically offering the same opportunity twice, so members could come to the one most convenient for them.

The first of these open discussions was very low-key. Perhaps twenty people were there, and most of the questions were about the logistics of becoming RIC: what it would mean for us and what specifically would have to change. The only thing that came up that was even a little controversial was the question of whether "marriage" was the right word for blessing a union between same-sex partners. The people gathered there seemed to have no problem with the church providing such blessings, but a few people had some misgivings about the language. And they were open to dialogue about it. Honestly, this was the kind of conflict I could deal with. The core group and I felt very confident and relieved after this discussion.

We went into the second open discussion expecting much of the same. It was after worship on a Sunday morning in the church fellowship hall. Debra stood at a lectern, and everyone else was seated around tables. I was at the back, with a notebook in front of me so I could take notes. I was sitting next to our minister of music. Before the meeting started, I kept writing things like "keep your mouth shut" and "just listen"—notes to myself.

About thirty or forty people were now seated around the tables. Debra opened the meeting with a prayer. She asked if anyone had any questions about the process.

A hand went up. "I don't understand why we have to do this. We're already welcoming to everyone."

Debra responded, "Yes we are, and this is a way we can show that to the LGBTQ community! This will help them know that we mean it."

Another question came. "But isn't this actually excluding people? If we say we're welcoming to gay people, don't we have to also say we're welcoming to black people and handicapped people and so on? Won't they feel excluded if we don't?"

Debra said, "Hmm. That's interesting."

Susan was sitting in the front row and stood up. "You know, we actually thought about that, about having our welcoming statement include a broader range of people." She looked at the questioner. "We could absolutely add that in. Would that help you feel more comfortable adopting this statement?"

The questioner rather feebly said, "I guess."

Someone called out, "Isn't the Bible pretty clear about this?"

Debra asked the questioner, "Did you attend the pastor's Bible study about that, the one he offered three times?"

The questioner said, "No, I didn't. But isn't the Bible pretty clear about this?"

Debra asked, "Did you read the pastor's article he wrote about it?"

The questioner said, "No, I didn't. But isn't the Bible pretty clear about this?"

I was having a hard time keeping my mouth shut. I called out, "No. It's not. But it's beyond the scope of this meeting to discuss why. I'll offer the course again if you like."

This meeting was not going the way any of us had expected.

Someone said, "You keep talking about welcoming people here. Well, I don't think this is very welcoming to people who don't agree with you!" There was a murmur of agreement throughout the crowd.

My temper was starting to rise.

Someone said again, "Why do we have to do this? Everyone knows we're welcoming to everyone."

I couldn't stay quiet any longer. I stood up and walked up to the podium. Every eye was on me. I said, "Every congregation in the world says that they welcome everyone. But people in the LGBTQ community have learned over the years that they're not welcome in a lot of those churches."

The questioner said, "But we are welcoming. Why do we have to go and tell them that?"

I said, "Because they think we're lying!"

Someone said, "Then I think that's their problem, not ours."

Someone else pointed at me and said, "Are you saying that we're liars?"

I stood there. I had no idea how to respond to that. I sighed, and my shoulders slumped. "No, of course not. I just . . . I don't know." I walked back and sat down next to our minister of music. She was crying. I put my hand on hers.

There was so much bullying. So much shouting. So much self-righteousness. Someone said, "I don't understand. Why can't they just come and not flaunt it? It's not my business if someone's gay unless they're broadcasting it."

I'd heard this argument before, but never at Living Grace. It meant that we're happy to welcome anybody, as long as they act like us. As long as they hide their differences. And it made me so angry in that moment. I stood up. "Well, if we don't want people to flaunt what they do in bed, then I'm going to have to stop talking about my children, because whenever I talk about them, it means I've had straight sex!"

There was silence. I heard somebody whisper, "That was inappropriate."

The meeting ended with everyone irritably agreeing to disagree. And the irritability stayed and spread. I started to hear stories about how someone in the church had told someone else, "If you don't agree to become RIC then you're not a good Christian." I heard stories about people predicting the end of the congregation. That whichever way this went, we were going to lose half our members. That we never should have started talking about this in the first place. Morale at the congregation was getting nasty. Worship attendance started to drop, and I heard stories that some people were not attending anymore because they didn't want to deal with the controversy.

I publicly apologized for the way I spoke at the second meeting. I tried to be clear that I was not apologizing for my beliefs on the matter but for the way I let my emotions affect the way I presented those beliefs. Finally, a straw poll was taken to find out the temperature of the whole congregation on the question. The plan was to use the straw poll results to decide on next steps before eventually bringing the matter to an official vote. The RIC core group had announced that they wanted a ninety percent majority on any official vote in order to adopt the RIC designation. Otherwise there would be too many people against it for us to really be welcoming.

Well, the straw poll came back at seventy-five percent positive. Way below what they were looking for, but nonetheless a clear majority. This meant that they really had to keep going and working on this. And nobody, nobody at all on either side was happy at this point.

I sat in my office at the church, staring at the wall. I could feel a familiar squeezing feeling at my temples, a gripping, wrenching feeling in my chest. I put my head down on my desk.

The voice in my head started. *This is all your fault.*

"I didn't start this. It wasn't my idea. They wanted to do this."

But you agreed to it. You allowed this to happen.

"There's nothing I could have done differently. There's nothing I should have done differently."

Incorrect. Your leadership style is obviously wrong. You should have been clear with your opinions from the start. Or you should have kept your opinions to yourself. Whatever you should have done, it's not what you did.

"How could I have known?"

You're smart. You should have known better.

"I am ruining this congregation."

You should have known better.

"I never should have come here."

You should have known better.

"I never should have been ordained."

You should have known better.

"I never should have been born."

Cut your losses.

I sat at my computer at home, researching a career in what was called geographic information systems. It sounded interesting and came with less conflict. I even enrolled in an online program to get a GIS certificate. But then I started thinking about what a career change would mean for my family. We'd have to move out of our home because we lived in a church-owned parsonage. We might even have to move out of the area or out of the state, depending on where the GIS jobs were. (Or at least I would have to move.) We'd take a substantial pay cut, at least for a while.

I said, cut your losses.

I started to think about all the work and time and effort that would go into this, all the sacrifice that my wife and kids would have to make. And then I remembered my life insurance policy.

There you go. Cut your losses.

I dug through the file cabinet until I found the policy. I read through it and realized that my death would solve all of these problems. No more ruining congregations. No more financial worries for the family. And no more pain like this.

I started to write suicide notes to my wife, my kids, and to the congregation.

I was driving over the Blue Mountain one day on my way to visit a parishioner in the hospital. As I drove down the north side of the mountain, I looked to the right and saw the steep decline just off the road. I felt the car inching toward the guardrail. With a quick turn to the right, I'd go careening into the ravine. I gripped the wheel, praying for strength. It would just take one quick jerk of the wheel. Just one quick jerk. Just one quick jerk. I sighed. Not today. Not quite yet.

I was walking across a footbridge over the Delaware River on my way to visit a parishioner who lived just a block from the bridge on the New Jersey side. I stopped halfway over the bridge and looked down into the water below. Was it deep enough? What about the rocks below? Were they sharp enough? I knew people had died there before. I stood there, communion kit in one hand, the other hand holding the handrail. I could just climb over. It would take moments. I sighed. Not today. Not quite yet.

I was standing in the bathroom just before bedtime. I was the only one awake in the house. I opened the pill container and popped my antidepressant into my mouth. I looked in the bottle—about ten pills left. I wondered what a lethal dose would be, or what I might combine with them? Would ten pills and a bottle of wine do?

A strange, dark calm came over me in those days. I knew that this was right. It was like freshman year all over again. Those same emotions, similar thoughts, all coming together in a nasty, self-destructive blanket of knives. History was repeating itself, and maybe this time I'd finally do what I should have done all those years ago.

There you go.

This was it. The end of my world.

INTERRUPTION
WORLD WITHOUT END

AGE 1 MONTH, 1 WEEK, 1 DAY

"The end of my world," I said. The Dark Voice agreed with me.

Then, a dream came. Or a reminder. Or a new message. Whatever it was, it was transforming.

I am in a large room. Windows with many colors on them. People, lots of people. They seem happy to see me. A few are in white robes. I am an infant in my mother's arms.

"Dearly beloved: Let us call upon God the Father, through our Lord Jesus Christ, that of his goodness and mercy he will receive this child by baptism and make him a living member of his holy Church."

One of the men in white robes is talking. I shouldn't know what he's saying; I don't know English yet. He touches my forehead, draws two lines on it with his finger: one up-and-down, the other left-and-right.

"Receive the sign of the holy Cross, in token that henceforth thou shalt know the Lord and the power of his Resurrection, and the fellowship of his sufferings."

I start to fuss. What am I supposed to be doing here? My mother tries to soothe me. She rocks me. She whispers to me. "It's okay. It's okay." But I am anxious, fitful. I hear only snippets of the liturgy going on around me.

"Since in Christian love you present this child for Holy Baptism, I charge you that you diligently and faithfully teach him . . . that, abiding in the covenant of his Baptism and in communion with the Church, he may be brought up to lead a godly life until the day of Jesus Christ. I therefore call upon you to answer in his stead:

"Do you renounce the devil and all his works and all his ways?"

I cry loudly. My mother and father speak together: "I renounce them."

The dialogue continues. I still hear only snippets.

"Do you believe . . ."

"I believe."

" . . . suffered under Pontius Pilate, was crucified, dead, and buried: Descended into hell . . ."

"I believe."

" . . .the Forgiveness of sins . . ."

"I believe."

" . . . grant unto this child now to be baptized, the fullness of thy grace . . ."

"Amen."

Then suddenly I am no longer in my mother's arms. I am held by another.

"Michael Joseph, I baptize thee: In the Name of the Father, and of the Son, and of the Holy Ghost. Amen."

I am handed back to my mother, but there is a hand on my head.

"Almighty God, the Father of our Lord Jesus Christ, who hath begotten thee again of Water and the Holy Ghost, and hath forgiven thee all thy sin, strengthen thee with his grace unto life everlasting. Amen."

Forgiven. Strengthen. Grace. All these words sound familiar, but I do not know them now.

" . . . through Jesus Christ, thy Son, our Lord who liveth and reigneth with thee and the Holy Ghost, one God, world without end."

World without end. Is that what he said? World without end?

PART FIVE
BE STILL

CHAPTER 33
HOW TO CHANGE A TIRE

AGE 40

A voice spoke to me, almost a whisper.

"There is another way."

I didn't hear the voice at first. I was overwhelmed by the other one.

Cut your losses. You should have known better. You are worthless. Just do it now—end it. It is a far, far better thing for you to do today than ever before.

That familiar voice. That terrible, treacherous friend who has echoed in my skull my whole life. But along with that voice was another—a voice so small, so quiet, yet so very, very steadfast:

"There is another way."

As summer waned and autumn arrived, I grew more and more desperate. I would stand at my seat near the pulpit, singing a hymn with my congregation, but inside I trembled as I thought, *This is it. I won't be doing this much longer. I'll miss this.*

I sat on the floor of my living room with my daughter. She was concentrating and writing as I read spelling words to her. I looked at her blond hair and that cute way her face scrunched up as she was thinking. I fought back tears as I thought, *This is it. I won't be doing this much longer.*

I didn't want to die. I didn't want to lose these things. I was so scared of leaving, so scared of losing, and so scared of dying. But I didn't see any other option. It was leave the church or leave the world. And I couldn't handle either one anymore. I was broken. I was useless. I had made things so very, very bad. But at the point of desolation, I found grace. And grace told me:

"There is another way."

I was listening now. I had nowhere else to turn.

"You don't need to leave forever."

What?

I was walking through the woods at a nearby park. I had been keeping my eye out for a good tree with a good sturdy horizontal limb not too far from the ground, when I heard it whispering through the breeze.

"You don't need to leave forever."

I kept walking as my boots squelched through the mud of a puddle in the trail. *I could leave the church, but come back?*

"Could you?"

I heard a red-tailed hawk somewhere in the trees, crying out. *Like a sabbatical?* I hadn't been at Living Grace long enough for a sabbatical. *I don't think they'd feel it was the right time for it, anyway.*

"Feel? How do *you* feel?"

I came into an area with very large trees that were spaced apart, a kind of wooded clearing. The ground was covered in orange leaves. I stopped and stared because the sun was refracting through the trees in a magnificent way. The amber light splintered into a thousand pieces through the leaves and branches, and the world around me had a warm orange glow.

"How do you feel?"

How do I feel? I feel like garbage. I feel—oh, right. I'm sick. I'm sick. This is depression. And if this is depression, if this is sickness, then I need care. What if I could take some time off as a medical leave?

I sat down and felt the leaves crumble and crinkle under me. I lay down, and just let the light wash over me.

The next day, I had an appointment with my current therapist, Dave, and I told him how I was feeling. "What do you think about asking for a medical leave?"

He nodded and said, "Well, it's pretty hard to change a tire while you're driving the car." We talked about what a medical leave might look like, what I might do during time off. It could be a time to get my brain back together and discern whether or not I could continue in this career or not. At least give God this one more chance to show me some hope.

I called the president of my congregation council as I left my therapist's office and asked her if she was available to meet with me. She was, so I stopped at her house on the way home. She offered me a cup of coffee when I arrived.

"Thanks for meeting with me today," I said. I swallowed hard. "This is hard to talk about, but you know that I've always struggled with depression. It's gotten really bad the past few months. I think it started with the way the Reconciling in Christ process has been going. But it's turned into something really bad in my head. I feel broken. I feel like I just can't continue. I've been honestly considering leaving the ministry. And I was wondering what you would think about the possibility of me taking a few weeks or months off as a medical leave so I could focus on my mental health."

I felt so vulnerable, so needy. I didn't like this feeling at all. But after a moment's pause, she looked at me and said, "Yes. Of course. You need to get better." She smiled kindly. "You do so much for us. Let us do this for you."

It was like that light from the woods shone on me again. We talked then about some specifics, how we might get this medical leave accomplished. The first step was to talk to the Mutual Ministry Committee.

A Mutual Ministry Committee is a special group of people within the congregation who meet quarterly with the pastor. It's intended to be a safe and confidential place for the pastor to share with a group who can offer the pastor support and feedback. I called a meeting with them and told them the same thing I'd told the president. By now I'd drafted out a plan which would include weekly therapy sessions, finding a spiritual director, visiting with my doctor to rule out any physiological problems, exploring meditation, and possibly even a partial hospitalization at a behavioral health center nearby. I was hoping for two months to accomplish this.

I shared all this with the committee as we sat around one member's kitchen table. They listened. They asked clarifying and compassionate questions. They decided that they would take this plan to the congregation council to ask for their approval. They were going to take care of this, not me. I felt that orange light from the woods again.

When the council meeting came, members of the council were just as supportive as the committee was, and they even expanded the committee's recommendation. I was offered three months medical leave with full salary and benefits. There was no squabbling over these things, no questioning if I deserved this. They saw my need, and they answered it in a way they knew how to. They were living their values; they were living as a sign of Christ's compassionate love. And I felt grace. I felt supported. I felt loved.

I was going to begin this leave on January 1. That was still six weeks away, but I wanted to get through Christmas, and there were a few other things I wanted to get squared away before I left. Since the worst part of my feelings was a sense of being stuck, just knowing this was coming was enough to get me through six weeks. I let the congregation know what was happening. I was so grateful that I had been so up front with my illness from the beginning because nobody was stunned. Surprised, yes. Concerned, yes. But not stunned.

I certainly don't know what went through the heads of everyone, but all the people who spoke to me seemed completely supportive. This was the same congregation that just a few months earlier seemed to be falling apart. This brought them back together. I lined up supply preachers and pastoral care providers so the congregation would have coverage while I was away.

And then January 1 arrived. I was off. Ninety days to try to fix this tire.

CHAPTER 34
DARK NIGHT

AGE 41

There were several acres of woods right behind my home. They were owned by the church, and I liked to spend time in them. My first two years at Living Grace, I blazed some trails and built a fire pit. It was a good place to sit and think and pray.

It was the evening of January 2, the first full day of my medical leave, and I built a fire. It was a cold day, but there was no snow on the ground. Sitting next to the fire alone with a beer in my hand was comfortable. It felt right. It felt real. And it gave me the chance to explore the feelings I had about this medical leave I'd just started.

I watched the flames flicker like tongues from the earth. I jumped a little when I heard the pop of a cracking log. I thought about Christmas. I thought about the previous morning, my last morning leading worship for three months.

In the secular world, the day before was New Year's Day, but it was still Christmas in the church year—the season doesn't end until Epiphany on January 6—and the place was still decorated gloriously for Christmas. After singing the final hymn, "The First Noel," the congregation walked out, everyone shaking my hand as usual. But so many people said kind things.

"I'll be praying for you, Pastor."

"If you need anything, just call."

"I'll be keeping you in prayer."

"We will miss you. Get better."

"I'm praying for you."

So many people told me they would be praying for me—so surreal, in a place where just a few months previously I felt like some were *preying* on me. I went back to my office, took off my vestments, double-checked my desk for the eighteenth time, and left.

And here I was, thirty-six hours later, sipping beer at this fire. Somebody asked me yesterday what my favorite Christmas movie was, and I answered *It's a Wonderful Life*. I was surprised by my own answer—I didn't realize how much I liked that movie. I thought about it as I stared into the flames. I thought about George Bailey, a leader in his community who was racked with guilt for mistakes he'd made and who realized he was worth more financially to his family dead than alive. So he made a suicide plan. Meanwhile, the whole town knew something was wrong with George, and they prayed. God heard those prayers and sent an angel to stop George and show him the way. And the angel, Clarence, worked a miracle.

I stared deep into the glowing embers as I recognized my own story. No wonder I had answered like that yesterday. And then I realized that I was expecting a miracle. I was looking for my own Clarence, my own personal angel, to show up and lead me on a journey for those ninety days, a journey that would bring me to an epiphany.

I needed Clarence because I was scared. Scared that I wouldn't accomplish anything. Scared that I would end up treating these three months as an extended vacation and just read and build fires and play games the whole time. Scared that anything I would learn through therapy and spiritual direction would just add to the pile of stuff I already knew and wouldn't change anything. Scared that I'd get back to church in a few months refreshed and ready to go, but the moment the chips fell again, the same thing would happen. Scared that I would learn nothing in the long run and that all this was for nothing. Scared that I was wasting the church's money, time, and prayers.

I thought again of the previous day's worship, how I had baptized twin boys. How I had told them that their baptism gave them a purpose in life, a meaning, and a role to play. (On days when I baptize infants, I always frame my sermons as though I am talking to the babies. I doubt they can understand me, but it enables me to connect with the rest of the congregation in a different way.) But did I believe that this was true for me? I was baptized too, but here I was, so uncertain of my own purpose, my own meaning, and my own role. I was baptized as an infant as well. I knew where it had occurred, and I knew that it was done using the old Service Book and Hymnal, the "red book" with its King James-style "thee" and "thou" wording.

I thought of Martin Luther, who was also a baby when he was baptized. He is said to have taken his own baptism so seriously that in times of distress or anxiety, he would find comfort by shouting out, "I am baptized!"

I tried it. I stood up next to the fire and shouted into the woods, "I am baptized!" No reply. No particular comfort. How did Luther have such faith?

I remembered the story of John the Baptist, who was out in the Jordan River baptizing folks to prepare them for the coming of the Messiah. John told the crowds, "I baptize you with water, but one greater than I is coming after me. He will baptize you with the Holy Spirit and with fire!" Here I was, sitting in front of the fire, but where was the Holy Spirit? Would I be baptized anew by the Spirit during these months? Would I feel that fire burning within? Was God really still here with me? I wasn't feeling despair—these were honest questions. I wasn't sure, but I hoped to God I'd find out soon.

CHAPTER 35
THE TEXTURE OF DEPRESSION

AGE 41

By now I'd been seeing my third therapist, Dave, for a few years. He had seen me through some ups and downs, and I had gained a lot of trust in him. During this medical leave, we planned to meet weekly, and I was hoping he would give me some tasks or even some overall direction for this time. (I was hoping he'd be my Clarence.) What he did instead was help me to see that I did indeed have a plan already, even if it was just little pieces of one, and that those pieces would come together if I paid attention. In order to help me pay attention, he encouraged me to look into mindfulness, a deliberate way of being aware of what's going on around and within you.

I started by reading a couple of books on mindfulness: *Wherever You Go, There You Are* by Jon Kabat-Zinn and *Mindfulness on the Go* by Jan Chozen Bays. I didn't stop at mindfulness; I looked into full-on meditation. I downloaded a meditation app for my phone. I started trying to meditate for thirty minutes a day. I found it surprisingly easy to do, at least when I had all this time on my hands.

I also read about various mindfulness and meditation exercises. I was surprised because I'd always thought that meditation was about trying to clear your mind of all thought. But there were other forms of meditation, other things to try. You can create a scene or an image, and focus on that, seeing where it takes you, where the scene flows. One such exercise asked me to consider in my meditation what my depression felt like. I wrote this after the exercise:

> What does depression feel like? I slowed down, focused on my breath, and pictured myself in a vast room, all alone, with a lit candle at the center (as the exercise suggested).
>
> I ask into the room, "What does my depression feel like? What is it? What are you?"
>
> In answer, I feel a presence come into the room from all sides, slowly, quietly crawling up walls that I hadn't even known were there. It is like a film clinging to these walls, everywhere but nowhere. It is dark gray and gritty, slowly turning this room into something that feels like a dungeon. I reach out to touch one of the walls, but I pull back immediately. It feels wrong; my fingers are too sensitive to its touch.
>
> I am reminded of a problem I have in real life—an aversion to terra-cotta. I am repulsed by touching anything like terra-cotta. I hate touching flowerpots. I have

a hard time holding chalk. It sends a shiver through my whole body. I have this strange fear that it will creep under my fingernails. The feel of the walls in this dungeon image is similar. A creeping, cringing feeling. I pull my hand away.

I sit back down and remind myself of the candle in the center. It is still there. I feel alone here, but on one level I know I am not. This candle represents my relationship with God, my relationship with other people, and my relationship with my true self.

My depression is a film that covers everything, but it is not me. I look up and see that the walls are dark and far away . . . the candle's light doesn't quite reach them. I instinctively know that this is because the walls are not real. The film of depression makes its own wall—it's a chimera. Beyond it is not an impenetrable barrier, but rather an open field. A field filled with light, the same light that shines from this unquenchable candle.

One day soon, I will see that field. One day soon, I will get up the nerve to poke through the flypaper mirage. One day soon, I will see that this dungeon isn't real. But not today. Today I sit here in melancholy contentment. It's okay. I've got my candle.

While the scene I described wasn't exactly happy, I felt at peace afterward. It was good to have this concrete way of seeing depression.

Another day, I meditated on God's grace. I considered the idea that grace is something we receive and then give away, like breath. You cannot exhale without first inhaling. You cannot inhale without first exhaling. Grace is the same. Or call it love. Or compassion. God uses our hands, our words, our bodies, and our spirits to share grace with the world. The grace that enters us is not a possession for us to keep. It's like breath, something to nourish us, which we then are called to send into the world. I believe that I am a conduit of God's grace. But what I cannot believe is that I am *worthy* of it. This image came to me through my meditation:

God's grace comes into me and then goes out again, just as it does through everyone else. But in my case, the path it travels is different. Because it does not reach my heart. Instead, it flows into me, and out of me into the world, but it is diverted within me. There is a kind of shunt that diverts it around my heart to make sure I do not receive any of the grace myself. I am grateful that I can be used by God in this way, but I do not experience the love. I have probably built this shunt myself because I do not want what I do not deserve.

The next day I was meditating on this again, and a similar image came, but this time it was grimmer:

Breath flows into my lungs, rich with life-giving oxygen. In the lungs, this air is transformed. The oxygen enters the bloodstream through the pulmonary vessels and is replaced by carbon dioxide, which is a poison, and needs to be exhaled. The process continues. Good in, bad out. Good in, bad out. The breath in and the breath out are not the same. Health in, poison out.

God's grace comes into me, but inside me it is transformed into poison: my heart alters it, makes it dark and wrong, and what comes out through my mouth is not what came in. And so the only way to ensure that God's love reenters the world without my poison is to somehow short-circuit the pulmonary exchange, so that what goes out is exactly what comes in. My lungs inflate and deflate, but they do not perform their life-giving miracle. They are no more than balloons, filling and emptying, filling and emptying.

CHAPTER 36

DARKWATER

AGE 41

I have almost no memory of the church where I was baptized or the town we lived in then. My family only lived there until I was four, and after we moved away, I only ever went back once or twice. But one day during my medical leave, on the anniversary of my baptism, I decided that it would be good to drive there. I wanted to check out the town, look at the church, maybe even go in, if it was open. I didn't know what exactly I was looking for, and to be honest, I was very disappointed with what I found: a bleak coal-region town and a locked church. No great epiphany. Just the thought that maybe this was my birthright—coal dust and boarded-up stores.

The next day, I had an appointment with Jane, my spiritual director. I had just begun meeting with her. A woman in my church who had some experience with spiritual education had recommended Jane to me. Jane was an Episcopal priest and a professor at a seminary not far away. When I'd prepared for this medical leave, it was important to me to work on both my mental struggles and my faith struggles. I would deal with the mental struggles with Dave, my therapist, and the faith struggles with Jane.

The plan was to meet with her every two weeks throughout my medical leave. I was still figuring out just what spiritual direction was. From Jane, I learned that it's a time of focusing deliberately on where God is active in my life, where God is absent, what God is up to, and how I might see that more clearly.

I told Jane about my trip to the church, and I told her how disappointing and disenchanting it was. Her response was to invite me on a prayer journey, which is a type of guided meditation. I closed my eyes and imagined I was back there again. I told her what I was seeing, and she asked me questions—pointed questions—questions about God's presence in all this. And I was able to see my trip in a completely different way. The result was a story I call "Darkwater."

> I walk the streets of this town, looking for signs of life. There is a main street with shops that advertise haircuts and guns, comic books and groceries. All are shuttered. The windows aren't broken, and there is no graffiti to speak of. I see no sign of crime or vandalism. But the stores are closed. It isn't fear that's closed these shops. It's loss: the lack of money, the lack of people, and the lack of life. The stores are there, but the people aren't.
>
> I continue to walk through streets of stand-alone houses and row houses. They are dirty. Dingy. Old. Every house has a porch, and here and there someone

is sitting on one. But mostly the porches are covered with rubbish: a broken chair, a rolled-up carpet, a few bags of trash. I walk past postage-stamp yards, and they are unkempt. I see broken cinder blocks and cement fragments. A tire swing that's torn and worn. This town is depressing and depressed. Coal dust and despair stick to everything. A high-rise looms above the other buildings, a place for the old and dying to look out over their old and dying town.

And there, in the middle of town, is the church. The old brick structure that I know is holy. I walk to the door. Locked. I peek in. The lights are out. Nobody is there. Pews sit empty. I sit on the sidewalk in front of the church, and I look around the town again, mentally exploring once more all the gritty nooks and crannies. I judge the people here and find them lacking. I say to myself, *These are not my people*, but a voice inside me says, "But you are *theirs*."

I put my head in my hands as I realize that this is a dream, and that in this dream, the town is *me*. This town is the core of my being. I belong here. This is who I am. I am depressed and I am depressing. I am dirty, unwashed, empty, and frightened of myself. Frightened and self-absorbed, broken and cracked, dry and unworthy of love. This is me—the me I try to ignore, the me I try to tell myself I've grown out of, the me I try to forget. But it all becomes clear in this moment. This is who I am.

I hear the sound of water off to my right and behind me. It must be the creek that flows past town.

They call it Darkwater—probably because of the dirt and dust it picks up as it meanders past. I turn to look at it, and I am shocked. I rise up from the sidewalk, rise up above the streets (I'm flying!), and I can see the river, for it is indeed not a meandering creek, but a rushing river. It is strong and mighty. It is clear and pure, and waves crest as it roars past. It is indeed dark, not because of dirt, but because of its depth. It is deeper than the world. Its bank is right at the edge of town. As the water splashes, it cleanses whatever it touches. All the dirt and all the dust is immediately washed away leaving clean sidewalks and green grass. This water is clean, pure, and vital.

I feel a tug, and I realize that I have been keeping it back. I have been holding the Darkwater at the edge of town. I have been preventing it from coming in for fear that it would wash me away. I loosen my grasp just a bit, and I watch as water flows into a few of the streets, cleansing them with hope and life. Nothing is washed away but the dirt. Life is returning. Life is growing. I notice that my hands are clenched, and I gently let them fall open. The water flows. Flows. Flows. Filling and renewing. Splashing and dripping. Pouring and laughing. The streets are clean. The porches are alive. At the high-rise, people lean out of their windows and cheer.

I turn to the church. The door is still locked, but there is a light inside. I peek in, and there are people there. I reach into my pocket because I know that there is now a key there. It fits the lock, and I walk in. The church is filled with people, dozens, maybe hundreds, maybe more. The pews they stand between face away from me, but the people have turned, smiling, to look at me as I walk in. They are all dressed in white, and I look down and see that I am as well. I look up and continue to walk in and find that they are not in pews but are standing in concentric circles with an aisle of sorts splitting the circles in half.

There is a place for me in the innermost circle, and I take it. I turn to the person next to me and say something. Perhaps it is, "I'm not sure what I'm supposed to be doing." Or perhaps it's, "I'm not sure what's going to happen next."

He smiles tenderly and says, "It's okay. Just be here." He takes my hand in both of his. These are my friends, my peers, my family. To them, I am not a child in need of wisdom. I am not an elder providing wisdom. I am not broken or cracked. And I am worthy of love. Simply because I am here. These are my people, and I am theirs. We all look up, toward the center of the ceiling of the church, and we smile in bliss. Before long, I find myself exiting the building again. The people wave to me as I go.

I am floating over the town now, and I see that it is dirty again. It is messy and awkward and hurting again. I look back at the church now and see that it is glowing. A golden light shines from within. The bricks are an amber brown now, pulsing subtly with life. And from the roof, a light issues forth heading straight to the heavens. It is a beacon. A beacon of hope and light.

The river is gone. It has done its work. Its rushing waves have filled the town and activated the light at its center. The town is still me. And I am still broken and cracked, depressed and depressing. That is real, and it is a part of who I am. But it is not all I am. I bear inside me now a thing that shines. A beacon that glows with light and life. The Darkwater has created the Lighthouse. The Lighthouse shines in the darkness, and the darkness did not overcome it.

There is a Lighthouse in the heart of my soul. I am baptized.

CHAPTER 37
ANOINTED

AGE 41

One Sunday morning I attended worship at an Episcopal church. I usually go to Episcopal churches when I'm on vacation or otherwise not working on a Sunday morning. Episcopalians are very similar to Lutherans; we're probably the two Protestant denominations closest to Roman Catholicism. (We might say we didn't throw the baby out with the bathwater—others might say we didn't go far enough in the Reformation. Your mileage may vary.) While the history of our two denominations is rather different, our theologies are very similar.

The teachings of the Evangelical Lutheran Church in America and the Episcopal Church are quite close in terms of how we talk about God, about the role of the church, and about interpretation of scripture. In worship style, we're almost indistinguishable, except that Episcopalian churches tend to be a little bit more on the high liturgy end. By high liturgy, I mean very formal worship with ornate vestments and incense and the "smells and bells" that some people love, and others loathe. Certainly not every Episcopal congregation has such high liturgy, and some Lutheran congregations do, but in my limited experience, Episcopal churches tend to be higher.

I have always preferred attending Episcopal worship to Lutheran when away for two reasons: first, I love high liturgy; second, I prefer to go outside the "Lutheran bubble" when I'm off. Especially if I'm still at home, it's nice to attend a church where I don't know the pastor at all and where I know that I'm an anonymous visitor.

So, there I was at this Episcopal church at its early 8:00 a.m. service. As I looked through the bulletin waiting for worship to begin, I was delighted to see they were offering the rite of healing near the end of worship. An invitation was extended to all who desired to come forward for laying on of hands and anointing with oil.

Anointing with oil is one of the most ancient rituals of the church, a ritual the church inherited from Judaism. In biblical Israel, kings and priests were anointed with oil, with whole bowls of oil poured over their heads to proclaim God's favor upon them. In the modern church, oil tends to be used more sparingly, but it is still important. In my own experience as a pastor, I anoint people with oil in three circumstances.

First, in baptism. In Holy Baptism, after pouring water on the head of the child or adult, I anoint the newly baptized by making the sign of the cross with oil on their foreheads with these or similar words: "You have been sealed by the Holy Spirit and marked with the cross of Christ forever."

Second, for healing. I have offered healing rites during worship many times myself. These rites do not promise a cure or physical healing. Instead, they are reminders of God's presence and of the wholeness that God desires. After laying my hands on the person's head, I make the sign of the cross with oil on their forehead, saying, "Receive this oil as a sign of forgiveness and healing in Jesus Christ."

Third, for a person's calling. On occasion, I have anointed people's hands at the end of worship and sent them out for service in the world.

As I sat listening to the rector's sermon, I was looking forward to the opportunity to be anointed in just a few minutes. I looked around the old, gothic-looking nave. There was only a dozen or so people here. No wonder—it was a rather snowy morning, and this was the early service. If this congregation were like most I knew, attendance would be much better at the later one, even on a day with good weather. But I always liked these early services: quieter, shorter, and fewer people. It fed my introverted side. I sat and listened. It was a good sermon on Micah 6. I recognized a good message when I heard it, but it wasn't quite the nourishment I was looking for that day.

A few minutes later, it was time to share the Eucharist. I followed the small crowd forward down the stone aisle, footsteps echoing off the high roof, and held my hands out to receive the gift of grace. I let the wafer dissolve on my tongue as I tipped the cup and sipped the wine. (The Episcopal Church, like the Evangelical Lutheran Church in America, practices Open Communion, which means that all baptized Christians of any denomination or background are welcome to partake.) Normally,

Holy Communion was the high point of worship for me, the moment when I felt most connected to God. That day, it felt just as good, but it also felt like it was just the appetizer—because I knew that anointing was coming soon.

After we had all sat down from Communion, the rector proclaimed the benediction and then walked down from the altar to the front of the aisle. He said, "Anyone who wishes to receive oil of anointing for healing is invited to come forward now." Interesting—it wasn't actually an integrated part of worship but just added on the end. I figured this was an artifact of the early service; I guessed it was included at a more organic time at the later service. But whatever—I was getting my oil.

I was sitting in the back, but I was the first to get up and walk forward. I didn't need to follow the crowd now. My footsteps echoed much more quickly on my way back up to the chancel. I felt my heart racing, knowing that this would be so comforting. I received even more than I expected.

The rector asked my name. He laid his hands on my head and said something like this: "Michael, I lay my hands upon you in the Name of the Father, and of the Son, and of the Holy Spirit, beseeching our Lord Jesus Christ to sustain you with his presence, to drive away all sickness of body and spirit, and to give you that victory of life and peace which will enable you to serve him both now and evermore." He then dipped his thumb in oil and anointed my head with the sign of the cross. And in that moment, I felt integrated, I felt whole, I felt holy. The moment I was anointed, I experienced all three forms of anointing: baptism, healing, and calling.

In the moment of anointing, I knew my baptism was renewed. The gift of life, the gift of hope that I'd received forty-one years ago as a five-week-old child was being renewed once more. The very same cross of oil was inscribed on my forehead again all these years later. The gift that my infant mind couldn't comprehend, the gift I still can't comprehend, the gift I saw in Darkwater, was made new to me.

In the moment of anointing, I also felt that it was God's will that I be healed. The priest knew nothing of me but my first name, but the God he invoked knows me, the God who had given me a new name forty-one years earlier in my baptism, the name "Beloved Child." Despite not knowing me, this priest could pray with confidence for my healing because he knew that it is God's will that all of God's children be healed. In that moment, in that precious moment, I actually felt that truth.

In the moment of anointing, I also experienced calling, being sent out to do God's work in the world. I had never experienced that in conjunction with healing before. The Episcopal *Book of Common Prayer* uses different words for the healing ritual than the Lutheran book does, and that difference was so powerful that morning. These were the words that hit me so powerfully:

> "... and to give you that victory of life and peace which will enable you to serve him both now and evermore."

Whoa. God wants to heal me not just for my sake but for the sake of God's work. God wants to heal me so that I can be a faithful, effective servant. God wants to heal me for the sake of the world. That was powerful to me because it helped me remember that I had a place in this world, that God wasn't done with me yet, and that I had a role to play. I didn't know what that role was exactly. But that day I felt—through that oil—that there was a place for me. Despite my illness. Despite my anxieties. Despite my doubts. There was a job for me to do. I was anointed. And the Dark Voice had nothing to say to this.

CHAPTER 38
HOME AT ST. DAVID'S

AGE 41

One Sunday during my medical leave, I went back to St. David's—the church where I had worked for five years as the director of Christian education, the church where I had the trouble with lock-ins. The congregation was celebrating its 150th anniversary, and throughout the year, they were inviting their former pastors back to preach. While I wasn't exactly a former pastor there (although I did preach about half a dozen times a year while I was there), they invited me, and I was touched. Of course I went.

The date I was scheduled to preach happened to be Transfiguration Sunday, the same Sunday that I "came out" to Living Grace four years earlier. As I prepared for this homecoming sermon, I thought that perhaps it would be appropriate to "come out" again since I'd never really done so at St. David's. I had of course shared a bit of my depression story with the confirmation class fifteen years earlier, but I never really talked about it openly with the congregation. Perhaps this would be an opportunity to do that.

The drive to St. David's took about an hour. It was my intent to drive alone. I left first thing in the morning so I could preach at the early service. My wife and kids were going to meet me there during the breakfast between the services and stay for the second service. I got in the car and looked behind me. My vestments were hanging in the back seat; I was going to wear them for the first time in about two months. I sipped my coffee and started the car. This would be a good time to be alone for a while. But I had a guest for the journey: I was about a mile from my house when he first opened his mouth.

Hey, remember how green and naive you were at St. David's?

"Of course I was. I was twenty-four when I got there, straight out of seminary."

What's your excuse for when you were twenty-nine and still there?

"Oh, stop it. I grew. I changed."

You were overconfident and arrogant from the day you got there until the day you left.

I pulled onto the highway. "There's some truth to that. But hold on. I made some good changes there. I had an impact on a number of young people."

Yes, but—

"But what?"

Do I have to say it?

"Shut up. I don't want to hear it." I glanced down at the speedometer. I was doing eighty. I did not intend to do that. I took a deep breath and slowed down.

Okay. I'll whisper it. Dave and Joe.

I looked down at the speedometer. Fifty-five. That's more like it.

I said Dave and Joe. You hurt them so much, remember? Do you think any good you did at St. David's could make up for that? And how about the pastor? Weren't you there to help him? A shame you just made his life harder. Remember that sinking, anxious feeling you always had whenever he called you into his office? That was a feeling you deserved.

"That's not fair."

Of course it's fair! You know what's not fair? The way you walked around there like you were God's gift to them, soaking up the adulation, all the while doing whatever made you happy.

I looked down again. Seventy. I breathed again. Fifty. The speed limit here is fifty.

"Yes, I made some mistakes. But I also did some things right, and I always tried to be faithful and honest. I tried to use my gifts to enhance the ministries of St. David's."

I looked around. This was so strange. I was heading into an area I had known so well just a few years earlier. I saw the boat store. And the ski rental place. A shame the sporting goods store had closed.

You know, you haven't preached in two months.

"I'm sure it's like riding a bicycle."

You're sure? And you know what else? This is an anniversary celebration. You know what they want to hear from you today? How great their church is. Celebrate it. They don't want to hear about your mental crap. Boo-hoo!

"It does feel a little self-indulgent to talk about my medical leave in this sermon."

A little? It's nothing but self-indulgence. Then again, why not? That's all you ever did here. All you've ever done.

"Now that's enough! Shut up!" I was speeding again. I was getting close now. I recognized the woods to my left. Back in 2004, I'd heard so many cicadas singing in there as I drove past that I thought there was construction going on. I wished they were there now; maybe they'd drown out this voice.

I slowed down and said out loud, "You know what? It might be awkward. It might be painful. But I doubt it. And I'm not going to listen to you anymore today. Enough."

I arrived about twenty minutes before the first service. The new senior pastor told me that many people were looking forward to seeing me today, that I must have made quite an impact while I was there. After chatting with him for a bit, we vested and got ready for worship.

It was a small crowd, much as I remembered for the 8:00 a.m. service. I recognized most of the faces but was surprised how many names I'd forgotten. Here are a few excerpts from the sermon I preached. (It should be noted that back when I was at St. David's, I developed a habit of preaching in verse sometimes.)

> And I hope you don't mind, but I'd like to discuss
> The disease that brought me to my knees
> It's something many of us hide in the dark places inside
> And I'd like to shine some light, if you please
> I live with depression, and sometimes it gets bad
> Medication and therapy help
> But something went wrong this past summer and fall
> And I could no longer do it myself

I'm learning to quiet the voices inside me
The voices that tell me I'm bad
The voices that tell me I should have known better
That help me feel worthless and sad

I'm quieting those voices, and you know what I hear?
I'm hearing a message come through
A message that I am God's beloved child
That God is holding me, saying "I love you"
It's a message of clarity, of seeing myself
The way that God sees me, I guess
It's not always easy to trust this message
To trust that God always says "Yes"
But I'm learning, I'm growing, I'm looking, I'm here
And every so often I see
A sign that I know must be from God
A sign that God really loves me

After the service ended, a woman approached me and told me about her own struggles with mental illness. She shared stories and worries. I offered to pray for her.

After I had spoken with her, I went into the Fellowship Hall where the breakfast was being served. When I walked in, there were already about a hundred people milling around. I recognized even more faces, including a few that I'd kept in touch with over the years. Many I hadn't seen in over ten years. I shared hugs. I shared small talk. I shared smiles. People told me I looked good.

They reminded me of some stories I'd forgotten. There was some good-natured ribbing, but nothing like what the Dark Voice warned me about. I had the opportunity to give a speech during the breakfast. Among other things, I talked about a man I knew at St. David's named Feryl. Here's an excerpt from that speech.

> One of the first homebound people I met here was Feryl, who was homebound because of his struggle with depression. I visited him and found him to be a deeply faithful, kind, and gentle man. He showed me pictures of his family and told me how proud he was of them. He showed me his backyard and told me how happy it once made him. He told me that he had built up a wall of isolation. He knew that there was such beauty and joy outside that wall, but he couldn't see it for himself just then. I heard so much about Feryl—the "old Feryl"—from other people: The old Feryl was full of life and joy. But his depression hid that person from the world, from himself.
>
> But a few months later, Feryl tried a treatment he hadn't had before, and a glorious thing happened. He found himself able to smile again. He found himself able to enjoy life again. I finally met the "old Feryl." He and I spoke frequently, and he talked often of his resurrection. He felt that he was doubly blessed because he would have the chance to be resurrected twice: once while he was alive, and once again sometime in the future after his death. Feryl died in 2004 after a long hospital stay, and his funeral was so holy. And I still remember the joy he had in the final years of his life,

the joy he attributed to God alone, the joy that he was given another chance at life.

My wife and kids (we were parents of two at this point) arrived during the breakfast, and people gushed over our eight-year-old daughter and toddler son. Afterward, I got vested again to prepare for the second service. As I expected, there were many more people there. Most people from the breakfast plus some other faces I knew and some faces I didn't. I preached the same sermon, and later there was more time to talk to people.

St. David's has a magnificent stained glass window at its front door, which is at the back of the nave. It's a huge red cross surrounded by a rainbow of colors. Light refracted through it affects the look of the nave as the sun moves throughout the day. To me, that cross represents the power and glory of God surrounded by an astounding diversity of light-bearers. It represents the church and the people of God who are so different and so beautiful as they bear the light throughout the world—the light changing as different people carry it in different circumstances. That was my experience of the people at St. David's that day as well. They were loving God-bearers. They had long since forgiven me for my faults and rejoiced instead in my successes. They loved me, flaws and all, and they shone the bright red light of that cross into my heart.

It was Transfiguration Sunday, and just for that one day, St. David's was transfigured and became home again. And perhaps I was transfigured too. I felt so very, very blessed.

CHAPTER 39
HIDDEN IN CHRIST WITH GOD

AGE 41

A friend of mine suggested that I consider taking a spiritual retreat at a monastery as part of my medical leave. She told me about a few monasteries she'd been to in New York State. After a bit of research, I decided to register for a program called "Living Hidden in Christ with God," a three-day, two-night retreat at Holy Cross Monastery. Holy Cross is a Benedictine monastery in the Anglican Communion (the Episcopal Church is also in the Anglican Communion, a bonus for me), located along the Hudson River in West Park, New York. A number of monks reside there, and the primary ministry of the monastery is to provide for individual and group retreats.

The monastery was a two-hour drive from my home, and as I drove there, I began to get more and more anxious. I started wishing that I'd never registered for the program. I thought that I should be home, getting stuff done. I felt that I should be anywhere else but on my way to the program. I didn't know what was expected of me. I didn't know if I'd fit in. I didn't know what I'd get out of it. I should have done more research. I should have figured all this out. I should have learned more about this. I should have, should have, should have.

You should have known better.

As I turned off the New York Thruway to get on the final roads, I thought about turning around. I was hoping that something had gone wrong with my reservation and that they'd tell me, "Sorry but you can't stay."

But I made it. The parking lot was just off the road, and the monastery was down a hill, a three-minute walk in the direction of the river. I walked down holding my registration papers, really unsure of what I was doing. The building loomed before me like some ancient dormitory, all red brick, steep roof, and windows.

I opened the main door, and a woman in a small office to the left greeted me. She asked my name, got my info, and told me what room I would be in. She said that Brother Roy was waiting across the hall to give me, and any others new to the monastery, a tour. I walked over to him.

Brother Roy was seated on a couch, dressed casually. He had a kind smile and a quiet voice. We made small talk—where was I from, what program was I here for, and so forth. After a few minutes, he said, "Well, I guess nobody else is coming for this tour. Ready?" He stood up and led me around the building.

He showed me the wide staircase that led to the small dormitory rooms. From there, he showed me the dining hall (refectory), a round room with a dozen or so tables and a buffet in the center. He led me into the common room, an eclectic space filled with mismatched chairs, couches, books, and games. We walked down a long hall, past the bookstore and the library, and entered the chapel. This was a cavernous space that smelled faintly of incense. The white stone walls curved delicately up to the ceiling. Pews for the monks were on either side, and seating for guests was in the back. In the center was a wooden preaching desk, and along the far wall beneath an enormous cross was a wooden altar. Light came into the room from high windows and from candles and old-fashioned lamps that hung on the wall.

The ceilings throughout the building were high, and I felt as though there was room to breathe and room for the Holy Spirit to soar and wander.

I thanked Brother Roy and settled into my room. It was small, with a bed, a desk, and a window. Nothing more than necessary. I unpacked, sat at the desk, and started to figure out the schedule for the week. I always did this when I was someplace new—I tried to get a handle on what the place was and what I was doing there. It gave me a sense of control.

Before long, I began to appreciate the rhythm of the place. It is based in great part on worship. The monks gathered in the chapel for worship five times a day for the "daily office": Matins (morning prayer), Eucharist (mid-morning Communion), Diurnum (midday prayer), Vespers (evening prayer), and Compline (night prayer). Guests are welcome at all worship experiences, and I took advantage of these opportunities. It was so deep and so holy.

Not only was there a rhythm to the day, but there seemed to be a rhythm to the church year as well. Each of the five offices (daily worship services) followed a particular pattern, but that pattern was adjusted based on the timing in the liturgical year, and also the day of the week and its relation to Sunday. I liked that. I resonated with the idea that worship moves in concentric patterns, around the day, around the week, and around the year. I imagine that over long periods of time, worshiping like this would yield a deep and subtle wisdom about the nature of time. And the chanting and the incense were like gold gilding the edges of a fine book. This was my kind of worship.

The retreat program had a rhythm of its own. There were three items on the schedule for our retreat, three items that repeated themselves many times. They were worship (in the chapel with the monks), teaching (in a large seminar room on the dormitory level), and meals (in the refectory). That's all it was. Worship, teaching, meal, worship, teaching, meal. (And some free time, and of course sleep.) It was all about feeding our souls, feeding our minds, and feeding our bodies.

It was a silent retreat, which meant that from the evening address on Friday to the morning address on Sunday, all attendees were expected to keep silent. Words of worship were an exception. There were about thirty or forty of us there, I think, but I never learned anyone else's name. I never found out where anyone was from, who they are in their normal life, how many kids they have, what they think of the weather, or what they think of politics. I didn't realize how much I dislike small talk with strangers until that small talk was taken away.

I could sit in the common area with my journal or a book, sipping my coffee, while a dozen others were in the room. I had no fear whatsoever of being interrupted. I had no anxiety about how much to open up to someone, how much to say, how much to keep silent. There are probably several good reasons for silence at a spiritual retreat. Dr. Martin Smith, the retreat leader, said that talking to one another could get in the way of someone's conversation with God and prevent a revelation that might be unfolding to that person. But I think for introverts like me, it's also just an awesome gift to be silent.

The theme of the weekend dealt with the depths of the mind. Dr. Smith said that neuroscience has shown that our true motivations, our true selves, exist deeper than we know, at a level so far hidden that we simply *can't* know about it. Our brains have layers of motivation and activity that are impossible to think about. Like an iceberg, a great deal of who we are is hidden from our conscious minds. And there are centers of the brain that do a very good job of weaving together narratives to make sense of what we experience. But that's all they are—narratives. The stories we tell ourselves about ourselves are not lies, exactly, but they have been shown not to be reliable. And so, *what is most true about us may be deeper than thinking can think, deeper than feeling can feel.*

But the point of the retreat was much more than the existence of our hidden selves; it was that *it is precisely in those hidden selves that Christ dwells.* Our retreat leader, Dr. Martin Smith, referred frequently to a few verses from Colossians:

> So if you have been raised with Christ, seek the things that are above, where Christ is, seated at the right hand of God. Set your minds on things that are above, not on things that are on earth, for you have died, and **your life is hidden with Christ in God**. When Christ who is your life is revealed, then you also will be revealed with him in glory (Colossians 3:1–4, emphasis mine).

If the most important and true part of our "self" is hidden, then the author of Colossians tells us that Christ is hidden there along with us. And through the act of *contemplative prayer* (a type of prayer that is similar to meditation, in which we attempt to quiet down our mind and our thoughts in order to connect with God), we can receive something Dr. Smith calls *intimations* (subtle hints, intimate signals) that come from God to us. These intimations tell us that our true identity comes from God and is promised through our baptism. They tell us that we bear the living Christ within us, and that when we focus on this connection, we can experience it.

This is the promise of the resurrection: not merely that we have been given life after death, but that the risen Christ has come into us, into the very depths of our being, a place that we cannot consciously connect to but a place that is very much there. This is not new wisdom, Dr. Smith reminded us. While science has only recently shown evidence of this "hidden self," Christian mystics, solitaries, and hermits have known about this for centuries.

This was a breath of fresh air for me. It reminded me of the image I received a few weeks earlier—the image of my breath being poison, that there was poison at my core that corrupted and polluted God's grace, so that what I exhale is no longer holy. But if Christ is *within* me, if Christ is *at my core with me*, then the breath that comes in as pure and rich is not tainted by me. Instead, it is replenished and revitalized by the Christ within. And what flows out of me is just as pure as what came in, refreshed and new.

In learning about the Christ within, I learned to *recollect*. In the context of this spiritual retreat, the word means to "re-collect," or to see the fragmented pieces of our lives collect together again. Of course, in common parlance, the word *recollection* means *remembering*. Look at the word *remember*—it's the same word as recollect; to re-member or to bring the members of the self together again. Dr. Smith said that this is what Christ does for us: collects our diverse parts and brings us back together. Christ is at our center. And when we focus on the center, we receive *recollection, remembering, and integration*—things we find so hard to come by in our fragmented, post-modern world.

As I reflected on this, I realized that this process was exactly what I'd been up to throughout my medical leave. I had been rereading old emails and old journal entries. I had been doing therapy work on old wounds and traumas. I had visited the place I was baptized. I had reconnected with some old friends. I was spending so much time remembering and recollecting things—and in the process, God was using these opportunities to re-member and re-collect my life.

CHAPTER 40
UNBIND HIM, AND LET HIM LOOSE

AGE 41

I returned from my medical leave at the beginning of April. It was an amazing homecoming. The Sunday before my return, I wore "civvies" and attended worship at Living Grace, just sitting in the pews with my family. The building seemed lighter. The people seemed kinder. The pastor who was supplying for me invited me to make an announcement if I wanted. I did, and I shared gratitude and hope. I told them a little of what I'd been up to over the past few months and told them that it had helped. It had really helped.

I worked in the office that week. I waded through hundreds of emails, piles of junk mail, and dozens of phone messages. Nothing urgent, nothing earth-shattering. Lay people had taken care of things while I was gone. But there was one distressing item: a letter that a member had written to congregation council in my absence about the Reconciling in Christ process. The president of council had left a copy of it in my mailbox. This member felt that council should not allow this process to move on, that it was tearing the church apart. I read the letter and felt my blood pressure rise. I felt the usual squeezing sensation around my skull and the clenching in my chest.

I closed my eyes and said to myself, "This is not my problem alone. This was not addressed to me, but to council. I don't need to solve this. The president shared this with me for my information. I don't need to fix this." I put the letter down and kept my eyes closed. I focused on my breathing. In, out, in, out. I kept this up for a few minutes until I opened my eyes and noticed that the sensations were mostly gone. I still wasn't happy about the letter, but it didn't feel like a tragedy, more like a nuisance. I smiled. I was better.

The following Sunday, I hung around in the narthex (vestibule) of the church for a while before worship just to have a chance to greet people as they arrived. Older members walked in, shook my hand firmly, and said, "It's great to have you back."

A young woman smiled and said, "Pastor, how *are* you?"

"Better," I said.

A few kids walked in and waved at me with big grins. "Hi, Pastor!"

About five minutes before worship began, I went back into my office to arrange myself. I clipped the battery pack of my microphone onto my belt and wrapped the mic around my ear. I donned my alb, snapping each of the snaps carefully. I tied my cincture around my waist with the special knot my colleague and friend Tony had taught me years ago. I slipped on my pectoral cross, the one St. David's had given me as a farewell gift so many years ago. And I put on my purple stole, the stole for Lent. I looked at myself in the mirror. I looked like a pastor. I looked like someone ready for this. I looked confident and prepared. So I guess . . . I guess I was.

It was the fifth Sunday in Lent when I returned, and the gospel reading assigned for the day was John 11, the raising of Lazarus. I stood in the middle of the chancel (the "stage" up front where the worship leaders are) and proclaimed the gospel from memory. One of my favorite things about this church building was how open the worship space was. I had so much room to spread out as I proclaimed the gospel. I stood at one end of the chancel at the beginning of the story then traveled across the chancel as Jesus and the disciples traveled toward Bethany, where Lazarus lived. I stood one on side as Jesus spoke to Martha, and on the other as he spoke to Mary. I was right in the center, standing beneath the huge cross hanging from the ceiling, as Lazarus came out of the tomb. Walking around this chancel felt free, like flying above the Darkwater Church.

Then I returned to the pulpit as everyone sat down for the sermon. It felt good to be back from my medical leave, and hearing the story of Lazarus again moved me to say something bold:

> *I know how Lazarus felt at the end of this story.* I know what it feels like to die and be brought back to life. I have experienced the power of death in my life, and I have experienced the life-giving cry of Jesus Christ saying, "Michael, come out!"

I can tell you exactly when that happened: January 25, 1976. I was just over a month old, and my parents brought me to the baptismal font at Holy Trinity Lutheran Church. And at that font, these words were spoken, "Almighty and everlasting God, the Father of our Lord Jesus Christ: We call upon thee for this child and beseech thee to bestow upon him the gift of thy baptism and thine everlasting grace by the washing of regeneration."

We used a different hymnal back then. If my baptism took place today, it would go more like this: Pour out your Holy Spirit, the power of your living Word, that those who are washed in the waters of baptism may be given new life.

And as the pastor poured water over my head, he said in the words of that old hymnal, "I baptize thee, in the name of the Father, and of the Son, and of the Holy Ghost."

I believe that at the same time, Jesus said these words: *"My beloved child, come out!"*

And my death was averted. My death was undone. I was but five weeks old, yet I was, like all of us, destined to die. I was, like all of us, already mortal, already broken, already sinful. I was, like all of us, heading for a future that would include suffering and worry, jealousy and anger, sorrow and disease. I was, like all of us, nothing but dust waiting to return to the ground one day. But on that glorious January day, Jesus called me out of the tomb and gave me life—new life, eternal life, full and rich life. And death would never have any power over me again. I was healed forever.

Now you might say, "If you were healed like that in your baptism so long ago, then why did you take three months for healing now? Why do any of us still suffer if baptism is that great?"

Good question. In fact, I think it's a similar question to the one asked in the story today. If Jesus loved Lazarus so much, why didn't he do something to keep him from dying? If Jesus is so great, if baptism is so great, why do we still experience suffering? Good question.

I think one response to that question is at the end of our story today. I think one response to that question is Lazarus himself. See him at the end of the story, standing in the door of the tomb. Yes, he is alive again, but he is wrapped from head to foot, with a kerchief over his face. Yes, he is alive again, but he is dressed like the dead. Yes, he is alive again, but death clings to him. Like death clings to us.

By the death and resurrection of Jesus Christ, we have been saved. We have been made alive. Yet death still clings to us. Death clings to us when we live with a physical or mental disease. Death clings to us when we love someone with such a disease, when we mourn the loss of someone we love, or when we mourn the loss of a relationship. Death clings to us when we face changes that are very difficult and when we live in fear or persecution.

Just as Lazarus was wrapped from head to toe in bandages, death clings so tightly to us.

And that is where the next words of Jesus come in. After Jesus called Lazarus to come out, he said to those around him, *"Unbind him, and let him loose."* Unbind him and let him loose.

This is what I have experienced over the past three months. People unbinding me. People unbinding the signs of death that clung so tightly to me, people unbinding my heart and setting me loose. You wonderful people of Living Grace, you have done that for me. My therapist and my spiritual director have done that for me. My wife and my children have done that for me. And others. Death had clung so tightly to me a few months ago, but now it is much looser. I have been let loose.

That is how Christ works. Christ calls to us and brings us life through the power of his voice. Come out!

And then throughout our lives, Christ continues to heal us, continues to unbind us from the clinging remnants of death, and he does that through other people. And that is what Christ calls us to do through our baptism. That is how we are called to use the life that Christ has given us. We unbind one another, loosen death's grip on each other, and set each other loose. Even though Christ has given us life, death always clings to us throughout our earthly existence. But together, we can loosen that grip. By showing compassion for the sick. Feeding the hungry. Welcoming the stranger who is different. Standing up for the oppressed and the persecuted. Proclaiming hope to the one who needs it. Forgiving one another. Giving generously of our time and money. And by praying, constantly praying.

And when we unbind another, we find death's grip on us grows a little looser too. This is the gift of baptism. Death will always be here, but Christ is stronger. Christ will always have life for us.

Amen.

EPILOGUE
THE THORN OF PAUL

Therefore, to keep me from being too elated, a thorn was given me in the flesh, a messenger of Satan to torment me, to keep me from being too elated. Three times I appealed to the Lord about this, that it would leave me, but he said to me, "My grace is sufficient for you, for power is made perfect in weakness." So, I will boast all the more gladly of my weaknesses, so that the power of Christ may dwell in me. Therefore I am content with weaknesses, insults, hardships, persecutions, and calamities for the sake of Christ; for whenever I am weak, then I am strong (2 Corinthians 12:7–10).

Paul never describes what this thorn is. Some have suggested it was a physical ailment of some sort. Some have guessed that it was epilepsy. Some have speculated that it was depression or some other mental illness. Some have suggested it was a reference to his critics, his enemies. It doesn't really matter in the end. The point is that Paul had something in his life that he found to be a torment, something he never wanted to live with. He prayed for this thorn to be taken away, but he heard God say to him, "No." Despite this, Christ used this thorn for good. In fact, Paul says, Christ was able to dwell in him more fully *because of* this thorn. Paul learned to appreciate his thorn. He even boasted of it, because he felt Christ's strength in him precisely when he was weak.

Based on his writings and on the description of him we see in the book of Acts, Paul was one of the strongest leaders of the early church. Without him, the church may never have spread beyond Palestine. Paul, the strongest of all, was so very weak and so very tormented. And he learned to appreciate that torment as a source of strength. Of course, Paul also really loved being locked in prison, so the guy clearly had his issues.

Depression is my thorn. The Dark Voice is the articulation of my thorn. It's been with me since childhood, it is still alive and well in middle age, and I have very little hope that it will ever leave. I'm not healed of my illness. The experiences of my medical leave at age forty-one didn't heal me any more than my eleven days at St. James Hospital healed me when I was seventeen. I still struggle. I still get incredibly sad and worried. I still give into the voice that tells me I should have known better. I still worry about what others think of me, and I still think about my own death more than I probably should. There are times when I still feel like the "Outstanding Boy" from ninth grade—like a fraud, an impostor.

But maybe that's the point. Maybe it's through this thorn that I am, paradoxically, strong. My openness about depression over the past few years seems to have become a source of hope, and indeed a sort of healing, for some people around me. God will continue to love me, broken as I am. Christ will dwell in my hidden places, broken as I am. The Holy Spirit will use me, broken as I am. If that's what it means for Christ's power to be made perfect in weakness, I can accept and embrace it.

This book is a memoir of the first forty-one years of my life, told from the standpoint of depression. I have shared the dark times, the rough patches, and the moments of desolation. But isn't it funny how those moments are so infused with hope, so touched with light, so immersed in the waters of baptism? Isn't it funny how it's in the darkest night that we see the clearest sign of light?

One of the blessings that Christianity offers me is an alternate identity. Instead of identifying myself by my mind and by my illness, I can listen for God's voice. God's voice speaks to me through my baptism, identifying me as God's beloved child. But that is hard to hold onto; it's as slippery as water. Sometimes it feels as though my mind is a battleground between the Dark Voice and the voice of God. And I never know who's going to win in the short run.

But there is hope. The arc of my faith story is long, but it bends toward hope. Perhaps that's true of all of us. There's a lot of suffering in the world, but there is hope. The Lighthouse shines from Darkwater Church.

ACKNOWLEDGMENTS

I could not have written this book without the help of many people.

The chapters of this book began as blog posts entitled "Snapshots of My Depression." Thank you to all those who read and commented on my blog at thescholtes.com, giving me the confidence that writing might be something worth pursuing. Special thanks to Cindy and Mary and Sherry, whose thoughtful comments so often went above and beyond.

Thank you to Pete, who gave me helpful commentary and support throughout my writing process.

Thank you to everyone at Boyle & Dalton for taking a chance on an untested writer with growing edges. Special thanks to my developmental editors Brad and Devon, for helping me to find the narrative within the stories, and to Emily, who patiently walked me through the publishing process.

Thank you to my wife, Heather, for helping me to make the time and space to write, and also for standing by me through so much of what I narrate in here. Thank you for being my heartbeat on the days when I just can't find it inside, for loving me even when I feel unlovable, for sticking by me through everything.

Thank you to the real people behind "Ryan" and "Amanda." Those two characters are composites of friendships I've had over the years. Thank you to Steve, Virginia, Kim, Jeff, Chris, Eric, Pete, Mark, and Amy Jo. I wrote about you—but you helped make me who I am.

Thank you to three of the best therapists in the world, Lucy, Steve, and Dave. You're all so very different, but each of you helped me in the right way at the right time. And thank you to my spiritual director, Jane: you took the raw material I gave you and helped me to find the darkwater in it.

I am grateful to the communities of faith I have been a part of throughout my life. Deep thanks to Prince of Peace, where I now serve as pastor, for allowing me to share my story honestly and openly, and for showing me that I can be weak and broken and also be a good leader. The seeds of this book were first planted in the three months you generously gave me to explore myself more deeply. Deep thanks to St. Andrew's, where I first explored how to be a leader, where I first explored how to share my story, where I learned to live out God's love. You, along with Pastor Dave Lutcher, believed in me and pushed me to be better. Deep thanks to Pastor Tom Neel and the good people of God Shepherd, for continuing that. Deep thanks to St. John's, where I grew up, the people who helped me to see what my baptism was and what it meant. And deep thanks to English Lutheran Church, the place I was baptized, the place it all began.

Thank you to Christy, my sister, for putting up with me while we were kids, and for becoming a source of support and inspiration in the years since.

Thank you to my parents, for doing your very best to raise me. I have no clue if you always made the right choices, but you always, always showed me love. You taught me about God's grace in so many ways, not least of which was this repeated sentence: "Michael, I love you, but right now I don't like you!" I pray I do as well with my kids.

And thank you, above all, to God, for creating me out of the dust, for breathing life into me. For washing me clean in the Darkwater. For shining that light in the darkness. For chasing me to that retreat center in New Jersey, and carrying me home. For never giving up on me.

ABOUT THE AUTHOR

Reverend Michael J. Scholtes is an ordained minister in the Evangelical Lutheran Church in America. He has served as pastor of several congregations in eastern Pennsylvania. Michael currently lives in the Lehigh Valley with his wife Heather and children Alex and Ben.

Keep up with Michael by visiting his blog here: thescholtes.com.

www.ingramcontent.com/pod-product-compliance
Lightning Source LLC
LaVergne TN
LVHW041539070426
835507LV00011B/829